Advance praise for
Surveying the Religious Landscape

"The patient, our nation, is very sick morally and spiritually. To anticipate healing, it is helpful to check the patient's vital signs, and no one can do it any better
than George Gallup. The patient is still sick, but there are encouraging new signs
of life. The sobering yet hopeful results of this outstanding study will challenge
us all. It is must reading for everyone who cares for our country."
> — Dr. Bill Bright, Founder and President
> Campus Crusade for Christ International

"Like Caleb who prepared the way for the people of God by scouting out the
land of Canaan, George Gallup, Jr., and Michael Lindsay have scouted the way
for the church approaching the new millennium. *Surveying the Religious
Landscape* is faithful to the high standards we've come to expect from The
Gallup Organization and is an invaluable resource for the people of God at this
historic moment."
> — Charles W. Colson, Chairman of the Board
> Prison Fellowship Ministries

SURVEYING THE RELIGIOUS LANDSCAPE

Surveying the Religious Landscape
Trends in U.S. Beliefs

George Gallup, Jr.
D. Michael Lindsay

MOREHOUSE PUBLISHING

Morehouse Publishing
P.O. Box 1321
Harrisburg, PA 17105

Morehouse Publishing is a division of The Morehouse Group.

Printed in the United States of America

Cover design by Corey Kent
Murnau Avec Eqlise II by Wassily Kandinsky, Stedelijk van Abbe Museum, Eindhoven/Lauros-Giraudon, Paris/SuperStock

Library of Congress Cataloging-in-Publication Data

Gallup, George, 1930–
    Surveying the religious landscape : trends in U.S. beliefs / George Gallup, Jr. with D. Michael Lindsay.
        p. cm.
    Includes bibliographical references.
    ISBN 0-8192-1796-4
    1. United States—Religion—Public opinion.   2. Public opinion—United States.
I. Lindsay, D. Michael.   II. Title.
BL2525.G36   1999
200'.973'09049—dc21   99-33214
                                                                        CIP

Contents

Graphs and Tables ix

Acknowledgments xiii

Introduction 1

Religion and Trends 7
    Importance of Religion, Influence of Religion, Church
    Membership, Church Attendance, Religious Preference,
    Denominational Affiliation, and Influence of Religion

Religion and Beliefs 21
    Belief in God, Miracles, Life After Death, Reincarnation,
    Primacy of God, Beliefs on the Bible, Beliefs Related to
    Science, Beliefs of Evangelicals, and Meaning of Life

Religion and Practice 43
    Prayer, Bible Reading, Religion among Blacks, Catholic
    Spirituality, Faith During Difficult Times, Charitable
    Contributions, and Religious Education

Religion and Experience 65
    Born-Again Experiences, Self-Reliance, Conscious of
    God, Developing Faith, Relationship to God, Spiritual
    Growth

Religion and Attitudes toward the Church 81
    Catholicism in America, Gays in Ministry, Organized
    Religion, Small Groups, and "Unchurched" America

Religion and Ethics 97
    Honesty and Ethics, Premarital Sex, Abortion,
    Presidential Ethics, Millennial Morality, Ethics without
    God, Physician-Assisted Suicide, Capital Punishment, and
    Situational Ethics

Religion and Society 119
    Religion in the United Kingdom, Religion in Canada,
    Religion in India, Global Family Values, Homosexual
    Marriages, Church and State, Race Relations, Care for the
    Poor, Confidence in U.S. Institutions, Ethics of
    Occupations, and Social Concerns

Religion and Youth 145
    Teen Church Attendance, Teens and Parents, Religion in
    Schools, Teen Beliefs, and Teen Religious Inclinations

Notes 165

Appendix 167

Graphs and Tables

Religion and Trends
Importance of religion remains high in the U.S. .10
Most believe religion losing influence 11
Seven in ten are church or synagogue members 13
Church attendance steady around two in five 15
Little change in religious preferences 16
Mainline affiliation dwindles 18
Two in three affirm religion's relevance 20
Religion and Beliefs
Americans' belief in God remains strong for fifty years 24
Percentage of Americans claiming belief in God or higher power 25
Miracles beyond 34th Street 26
Is there a heaven? 27
Two-thirds affirm life after death 28
Do you think existence in the afterlife is a positive,
    negative, or neutral experience? 28
Do you think of your existence in the afterlife
    as being a journey of some kind or not? 29
Do you believe that the quality of existence after death is
    different for different people or the same for all? 29
Is heaven something you believe in, something you're
    not sure about, or something you don't believe in? 30
Is hell something you believe in, something you're not
    sure about, or something you don't believe in? 30
Nearly one in three believes in reincarnation 32
Whose life is it? 33
One in three is a Bible literalist 35
Creation, science & the dinosaur 37
Nearly half are creationists 38
Extraterrestrial life stumps Americans 39
Surprising beliefs of Evangelicals 40
Public searches deeply for meaning of life 42

Religion and Practice

How Americans pray 46
What people pray for 47
Majority feel prayer important 48
Biblical trivia 49
America's most popular book 50
How often do you read the Bible? 50
People read the Bible to feel closer to God .51
How important is religion among black Americans? 53
Personal piety wanes among Catholics 55
Religion lifts depressed adults 57
People cope with crisis through family and prayer 58
Americans will give away property before time 60
Three-quarters of nation have been taught religion 61
Almost all want kids religiously educated 63

Religion and Experience

Born-again experience pervades 68
One-third of nation claim religious experience 69
Self-reliant people predominate 71
Nearly all sense presence of God 72
Religion's importance intensifies as people grow older 74
Many Americans desire to develop faith 75
Most adults interested in relationship to God 77
Four out of five need to grow spiritually 79

Religion and Attitudes toward the Church

Catholicism in American 84
Do Catholics agree with all of the church's teaching? 85
Two in three Catholics support women's ordination 86
Americans draw the line on gays in ministry 87
Organized religion takes its test 89
Group support 91
Strength in small numbers 92
Houses of worship fill a need 93
Widespread commitment to small groups of faith 94
Unchurched America has changed little in 20 years 96

Religion and Ethics

Americans bemoan sagging ethics 100
Majority say premarital sex not wrong 101
Faith molds opinions on abortion 103
Many approve of abortions in special situations 104
Eight out of ten value morals in presidential hopefuls 106

Morality increasingly important for U.S. presidents 108
Millennial morality 109
Ethics do not hinge upon religious faith 111
Public split on physician-assisted suicide 113
Religion has little impact on opinion of death penalty 114
Declining belief in situational ethics 116

Religion and Society
Is religion less important in Canada than in U.S.? 121
America surpasses other nations in faith matters by belief in: 122
British and American faith 123
India: as religious as America 124
Social values in India 125
No global consensus on family values 127
Most still disapprove of homosexual marriage 128
How much political influence do religious leaders have? 130
Discrimination: not necessarily a Black-and-White issue 132
One-half of Blacks experience discrimination 133
Incidence of unfair treatment in selected situations
        within the last 30 days 134
Americans think government should provide for the needy 135
Americans place highest confidence in churches 137
Trend of confidence in the church 138
Pharmacists, clergy are most highly-rated occupations 140
Clergy ratings 141
Citizens vote on social issues 142

Religion and Youth
More teens than adults in church today 147
Teens plan to be more religious and giving than their parents 149
The good ole' golden rule days? 150
Two-thirds favor prayer in schools 152
Will schools reopen to different school prayer practices? 153
Most Americans endorse religion in public schools 154
Views of public school students 155
87% approve of sex education in schools 156
Teens believe in the supernatural, not the paranormal 158
Young people mirror adult religious beliefs 159
Trends in teen religious behavior and belief 160
Religious preference in choosing a roommate 161
American teens claim to be religious people 162

Acknowledgments

From George

This project involved the work of several individuals whom I would like to thank. I would like to express my deep appreciation to Michael Lindsay for his total commitment to this book project. He has been an ideal partner in this effort to shed light on the spiritual condition of our society. Also, I am grateful to Marie Swirsky, my able assistant, who helped with the preparation of this manuscript as well as handled many of the logistical details for this project. Finally, thanks to Debra Farrington, Christine Finnegan, and their associates at Morehouse Publishing for their support and suggestions in bringing this project to completion. I am grateful to all of you.

From Michael

Sir Isaac Newton wrote, "If I have seen further it is by standing on the shoulders of giants." Through the preparation of this book, I have been blessed to stand on the shoulders of several giants. First, I want to thank Mr. George Gallup, Jr., for the opportunity to join him in this venture. It is an honor to be following along the path of religious survey research that he has been blazing for nearly a half century. I am also grateful to Dr. Gary Cook, another giant who has been a great mentor to me. His encouragement and counsel have bolstered my spirit many times, and I appreciate his continuing support of my calling and work on this project. Maura Strausberg and Lydia Saad, colleagues at The Gallup Organization, helped me gather much of the data for this text, and I thank them for their assistance and patience. My mother Susan sacrificed her Thanksgiving holiday to read this manuscript, and I greatly valued her thoughtful suggestions—as has been the case for all of my life. Finally, the preparation of this text would have been impossible without the sustaining encouragement of my greatest confidante and best friend, my wife Rebecca, to whom this book is dedicated with gratitude and love.

George H. Gallup, Jr., and D. Michael Lindsay
Princeton, New Jersey
December 1999

Introduction

One cannot understand America if one does not have an awareness and appreciation of the religious underpinnings of our society. *Surveying the Religious Landscape* is dedicated to this proposition.

For two-thirds of a century, Gallup and other polling organizations have sought to gain insight into the *minds* and *hearts* of the populace and, increasingly in recent years, the *souls* of Americans, certainly the most difficult task of all. Polling organizations already survey cross-culturally on many different "external" experiences. The continuing challenge to pollsters, sociologists, and others is to devise measurements that are useful for understanding people's "internal" experiences as well. And these, after all, are the most important for understanding and improving life on earth. The inner life is one of the new frontiers of survey research, in a new era of discovery—not of the world around us, but of the world within.

New attention is being given to what is called the "faith factor" in American life, with a mounting body of survey findings and data from other sources pointing to the power of this factor. The deeply spiritual or religiously committed among the American population have less stress and cope better with it. They have fewer drug and alcohol problems, less depression, and lower rates of suicide. They enjoy their lives and marriages more than do the less religious in society.

Surveying the Religious Landscape reveals the basic religious beliefs, practices, knowledge, and experience of the U.S. public, as well as their attitudes about the church, the state of morality in the nation, and a number of other topics.

In reflecting upon the survey findings under each of these topics, it might be useful for the reader to assess the religious or spiritual state of the nation on three levels: 1) spirituality; 2) support for the church and organized religion; and 3) sincere and transforming faith.

1. Spirituality.

The percentage of Americans who say they feel the need in their lives to experience spiritual growth has surged twenty-four points in just four years—from 58% in 1994 to 82% in 1998. The percentage that says they have thought a lot about "the basic meaning and value of their lives" has swelled eleven points—from 58% in 1985 to 69% today. Clearly, much is stirring in the spiritual life of the populace as we move into a new century.

Factors behind these remarkable trends likely include a rejection of materialism; a recoiling from the terrible examples of "man's inhumanity to man" seen in the wars of this century and in mindless violence; a growing conviction that humans left to their own devices will destroy themselves; and the belief that there must be something better ahead.

Some of this "new spirituality" may be reflected in continuing uptrends in religious indicators, including the growing percentage who say religion is important in their lives. Much of this spirituality, however, appears to be free-floating and vague and does not necessarily have an impact upon traditional religious beliefs. For example, when people are asked if they rely more on themselves to solve the problems of life or more on an outside power, such as God, the percentage saying self has grown nine points since 1983, while the percentage saying an outside power, or God, has stayed at the same level.

In the realm of experience, an extraordinarily high proportion of Americans, a net of 30%, report they have had at some point in their lives a "remarkable healing" related to a physical, emotional, or psychological problem. A total of 21% say a physical problem while the same proportion, 21%, cite an emotional or psychological problem.

Most (seven in ten) attribute the healing to supernatural forces, with 42% naming God or Jesus Christ or a Higher Power and 30% their own prayers or the prayers of others. Another 27% gave other responses. Most who claimed to have had a healing said that it made them more aware of the importance of their spiritual life (89% said this), and 84% said it deepened their religious faith.

2. Support of organized religion.

Judging from national findings on basic religious indicators of belief and practice, Americans today appear to be just as attached to religion as they were a half century ago. A total of 95% of the public in 1947 said they believed in God; 96% hold this belief today; 73% in the earlier survey professed a belief in some kind of afterlife; 71% do so in a recent survey.

In the matter of religious practices, 90% a half century ago said they prayed; the figure today is the same. Four in ten Americans in 1947 reported attending church "regularly"; the recent Gallup surveys reveal the same proportion.

The size of the segment of the populace that is unchurched tends to underscore the remarkable stability one observes in the overall national religious picture, at least in terms of the last two decades. In a 1998 survey, 44% fit the category of "unchurched," the same figure recorded a decade earlier, in 1988, and slightly higher than the percentage recorded in 1978 (41%). The unchurched are defined as those who are not members of a church or have not attended services in the six months prior to the interview other than for special religious holidays, weddings, funerals, or the like.

Although in general there appears to have been a flatness in overall national religious beliefs and trends over recent decades, it is important to note that certain major changes have, indeed, occurred—for example, in the percentage of Americans who hold a literal view of the Bible. Furthermore, the percentage of adults who state their religious *preference* as Episcopal, Presbyterian, or Methodist is one-third lower today than three decades ago. Losses for Lutheran churches over this period of time are less pronounced, and Baptists (Southern Baptists and other Baptists combined) remain at about the same level as in the late 1960s. In assessing the strength of a faith or denomination, it is important to measure *preferences* as well as membership, since most Americans, if they are not presently church members, have been so in the past or will be in the future.

3. A deep, transforming faith.

Although Gallup religious indicators reveal a continuing high level of attachment to religion, the same question persists: religion is broad, but is it deep? Evidence suggests that in both recent surveys and those taken a half century earlier, the percentage of the populace with a deep, transforming, lived-out faith is far smaller than the overall percentages on religious belief would seem to indicate.

The religious or spiritual condition of Americans today can perhaps be best described in terms of gaps. First, there is an ethics gap—the difference between the way people think of themselves and the way they actually are. Religion is highly popular in this country, but survey evidence suggests that it does not change people's lives to the degree one would expect from the level of professed faith.

Second, there is a knowledge gap—the gap between Americans' stated faith and their lack of the most basic knowledge about that faith. Finally, there is a gap between believers and belongers—a decoupling of belief and practice.

Millions of people of all faiths are believers, many devout, but they do not always participate in the congregational lives of their denominations. Americans tend to view their faith as a matter between them and God, to be aided, but not necessarily influenced, by religious institutions.

Furthermore, considerable overlapping is found in religious beliefs and practices. People tend to pick and choose the items of belief that best suit them. Reginald Bibby, the Canadian sociologist, calls this "religion à la carte." Substantial proportions of traditional Christians, for example, subscribe to non-Christian beliefs and practices, such as reincarnation, channeling, astrology, and fortune telling.

The picture of religion in America, as suggested by the findings in this book, is a complex one, but certain underlying themes emerge:

- The widespread and continuing appeal or popularity of religion
- The glaring lack of knowledge about the Bible, basic doctrines, and the traditions of one's church
- The inconsistencies of belief—for example, evangelical Christians expressing belief in New Age practices
- The superficiality of faith, with many people not knowing what they believe, or why
- A belief in God, but a lack of *trust* in God
- A failure on the part of organized religion in some respects to make a profound difference in our society, despite the fact that churches reach six out of ten Americans in a given month

Author and businessman Bob Buford, in his book *Halftime*, sums up the situation: "…most of us seem somewhere stuck between disbelief and the quiet confidence that comes from knowing God."[1]

Although faith communities perhaps sometimes fail to challenge believers to their calling, organized religion continues to play a major, pivotal role in U.S. society. What is much less clear—and far more difficult to predict—is the direction of religion in terms of the depth of faith. It is at a level of deep commitment that we are most likely to find lives changed and social outreach empowered. Will the nation's faith communities challenge as well as comfort people? Will they be able to raise the level of religious literacy? These are questions that need to be addressed by the clergy and religious educators of all faiths.

Two of the underlying desires of the American people at this time are to find deeper meaning in life and to build deeper, more trusting relations with other people in our often impersonal and fragmented society. If these desires are sincerely and creatively addressed, the vitality of America's churches could well be the surprise of the twenty-first century.

The faith communities of the United States face enormous challenges, but there are, at the same time, certain factors at work that can improve prospects for deepening religious faith. To a considerable extent, the soil has been prepared for a possible reinvigoration of religious faith. The U.S. is, for the most part, a "churched" nation. Most people attest to religious beliefs, adhere to a particular denomination, and believe religion is important. Most have had some form of religious training. Furthermore, the church or organized religion continues to be one of the institutions held in the highest esteem when compared with other institutions of our society; therefore, it can be expected to play a powerful leadership role in the future. Also, churches generally are regarded as having done a good job in meeting the physical and spiritual needs of people in a given community, and the clergy continue to be held in relatively high esteem. The vast majority of Americans believe in the power of prayer, pray frequently, and believe prayers are answered. The basic foundation for a revitalized faith therefore would appear to be in place.

And finally, another basis for encouragement is seen in the fact that the rank-and-file churchgoers appear ready to be called upon. In one survey we discovered that Americans by a six-to-one ratio said members should have greater influence in their churches. The ratio is yet higher among young upscale groups, who will provide a large share of the leadership of churches in the future.

Whatever strategies are developed to revitalize religious faith in our churches and in society as a whole, they should be considered with urgency. The observation that the church is "only one generation from extinction" applies today as perhaps never before.

Religion and Trends

In the seven decades of scientific polling (1935–2000), rapid and dramatic social change has altered the nation's religious mood, despite the remarkable stability of beliefs and practices among Americans. Although largely unchanged throughout survey history, mainline religious commitment was relatively low during the Depression years and the Second World War. Diverse movements such as neo-Orthodoxy, revival of the Social Gospel, and a resurgence of fundamentalism spurred religious interest in the years leading up to 1950.

In 1947 postwar recovery swelled church and synagogue membership to the highest level ever recorded by Gallup (76%). The ratio of Protestants to Catholics in terms of religious preference was far greater than today, with 69% of U.S. adults identifying themselves as Protestants and 20% as Catholics. In 1952, the year of Dwight D. Eisenhower's election, the trend peak of 75% nationwide found religion "very important." With the Cold War well underway, "In God We Trust" become the national motto. Church and synagogue attendance reached a high of 49% in 1955, matched in 1958. And, in 1957, with American civil religion approaching religious nationalism, 69% said the influence of religion on American life was increasing, compared to 42% in 1998.

The onset of the Vietnam War radically changed the mood that prevailed during the 1950s. By 1965, deep disaffection with the social order had given rise to a counterculture that embraced Eastern mysticism and the politics of a new left. Public confidence in American institutions declined sharply in the wake of violence across campuses and inner cities, as the civil rights movement began and the Tet offensive shattered expectations of a military victory in Southeast Asia. As for organized religion, however, membership, attendance, and the belief in the importance of religion fell, not only among Catholics but also among Protestants and Jews. National attendance at houses of worship dropped from 49% in 1958 to 42% in 1969, with the decline most pronounced among young adults (ages 18 to 29), down fifteen points, and among Catholics, down eleven points. In 1962, 31% nationwide felt that religion was losing influence on society, up seventeen points from 1957. By the end of the decade that percentage had climbed to seventy.

The early 1970s marked the breakdown of Americans' sense of national unity and ushered in one of the lowest points in public morale. The devastating loss in Vietnam followed closely by Watergate intensified disillusionment with government and institutions in general, and the effect on religious institutions lasted well into the 1980s. Churches and synagogues suffered serious declines in membership and attendance, with churchgoing at 40%, down by nine percentage points from 1958. The downtrend could be traced almost entirely to falling attendance among Catholics, whose 1973 attendance rate was 55%, down from 71% ten years earlier. Furthermore, at the outset of the decade, 75% suggested religion was losing impact and only 14% said it was gaining, percentages almost exactly reversed from 1957. In mainline communities, as the distance grew between a liberal clergy and a more conservative laity, both sides became reluctant to form a cohesive religious identity. Evangelical and revivalist churches, on the other hand, were advancing new members toward the cultural mainstream.

In 1976, Jimmy Carter entered the Oval Office as a born-again Southern Baptist Sunday school teacher supported heavily by an evangelical, Democratic constituency. By that year the slide of a decade and a half in religious involvement had leveled off. A marginal upturn to 42% occurred in weekly churchgoing, and membership steadied at 71%. The proportion of Americans reporting greater influence of religion grew to 44% and then to 49% in 1985, more than triple the percentage recorded in 1970. Religious pluralism flourished, with a projected 10 million in 1976 involved in transcendental meditation, mysticism, yoga, or Eastern religions, 3 million in the charismatic movement, and 34% nationwide calling themselves born-again or evangelical Christians.

Following the 1980 election of born-again Christian Ronald Reagan, optimism among conservatives reflected a discernable movement to the right in statements of faith among many major religious bodies. Attendance and membership levels remained stable, along with the proportion of 56% saying religion was "very important." But relocations away from liberal and moderate Protestant churches had drained their numbers during years of growth among Catholics, Southern Baptists, Latter-day Saints, and Pentecostals. Evangelical affiliation nationwide held steady into the early 1990s. By the time yet another born-again Christian, George Bush, won the presidency, the religious mood of the mid-1970s had given way to the climate of ambivalence that attends social transition and cultural change. Given the religious privacy in America today, Bush's inaugural call for voluntary public virtue and civil religious values may have reflected a broad but diffuse base of support for the nation's spiritual regeneration in the coming century.

When Bill Clinton clinched victory in the 1992 presidential race, he had been a long-standing choir member of a Southern Baptist congregation in Little Rock, Arkansas. Despite the openness with which he spoke of his religious beliefs, many religious conservatives disagreed with his policies and initiatives. His support of gays in the military and abortion rights angered many members of the Religious Right community. Tales of his extramarital relations—which took center stage in 1998 when he admitted to an "inappropriate relationship" with Monica Lewinsky—confounded religious advocates even further. However, during his administrations, support for religion's importance and relevance increased from the levels that existed prior to his election. While a majority of Americans continue to believe that religion is losing its influence in today's society, that percentage has slowly diminished over the course of the decade of the 1990s. Moreover, statistics for church membership and attendance have remained constant during the 1990s despite the growing skepticism and indifference to religious ideals that predominate the postmodern worldview.

For more than sixty years, The Gallup Organization has polled Americans' religious beliefs and practices. This section contains surveys that can be traced back to the 1930s, 1940s, and 1950s. In addition to offering the latest statistics, this section provides interesting highlights from previous years. Not all questions have been asked every year since the late 1930s; as a result, not every year is listed in the trend tables. Some responses do not add up to 100% because of rounding.[2] Also in a few instances, this text omits certain categories of data that are not necessary to glean the overall trends in religious belief that have occurred over the past fifty years. For more information on Gallup methodology, refer to the Appendix.

IMPORTANCE OF RELIGION

Three out of five Americans in 1998 classified religion as "very important" to their lives. This represents a seven percentage point gain since 1988. Belief in the importance of faith and religion ebbed around the halfway mark in the late 1970s. Throughout the 1980s, a little over half of the nation ranked religion as "very important" to their personal lives. Since 1988, however, the figures have climbed. In 1997 and 1998, in fact, they reached the 60% mark, which mirrors public opinion during the late 1960s and early 1970s.

Two out of three women in this country (67%) rate religion as very important. Among certain segments of the population, the level of support is even higher. For example, 85% of Blacks in the United States regard religion and faith as very important. Three out of four Hispanics in this country hold similar convictions. Noteworthy distinctions appear between different age groups in America. Although only 46% of the nation's young adults (ages 18 to 29) give religion top priority in life, 67% of adults ages 50 to 64 regard religion in the same way. The figures surpass 70% for adults over age 65. Adults ages 65 to 74 give the highest endorsement for religion's importance for a person's life. Nearly eight out of ten of them (79%) consider religion "very important" to their lives.

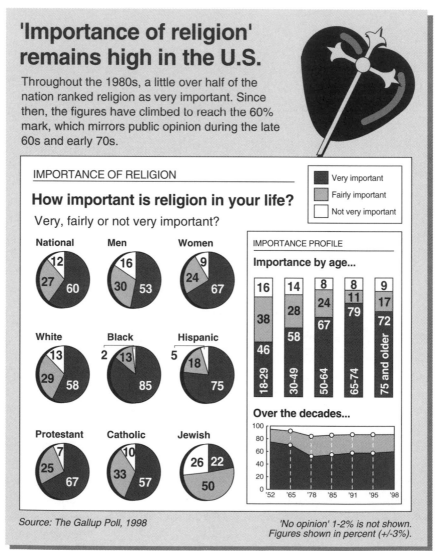

'Importance of religion' remains high in the U.S.

Throughout the 1980s, a little over half of the nation ranked religion as very important. Since then, the figures have climbed to reach the 60% mark, which mirrors public opinion during the late 60s and early 70s.

IMPORTANCE OF RELIGION

■ Very important
▨ Fairly important
□ Not very important

How important is religion in your life?

Very, fairly or not very important?

National: 12, 27, 60
Men: 16, 30, 53
Women: 9, 24, 67

White: 13, 29, 58
Black: 2, 13, 85
Hispanic: 5, 18, 75

Protestant: 7, 25, 67
Catholic: 10, 33, 57
Jewish: 26, 22, 50

IMPORTANCE PROFILE

Importance by age...

18-29	30-49	50-64	65-74	75 and older
16	14	8	8	9
38	28	24	11	17
46	58	67	79	72

Over the decades...

'52 '65 '78 '85 '91 '95 '98

Source: The Gallup Poll, 1998

*'No opinion' 1-2% is not shown.
Figures shown in percent (+/-3%).*

J. Farnell

Differing faith communities provide diverse responses on the matter of religion's importance. Two out of three Protestants (67%), for instance, evaluate religion as "very important" to one's life. Support rises to even higher levels among Southern Baptists (77%), Pentecostals (86%), and Church of Christ members (65%). Catholics, on the other hand, fall slightly below the national average with 57% of their members ranking religion as "very important." Only one in five Jews (22%) regards religion in this manner; 50% of them deem it "fairly important," while another quarter (26%) considers religion "not very important."

INFLUENCE OF RELIGION

Two out of five Americans assert that religion is gaining influence on American life. Within the thirty-year period of the 1970s through the 1990s,

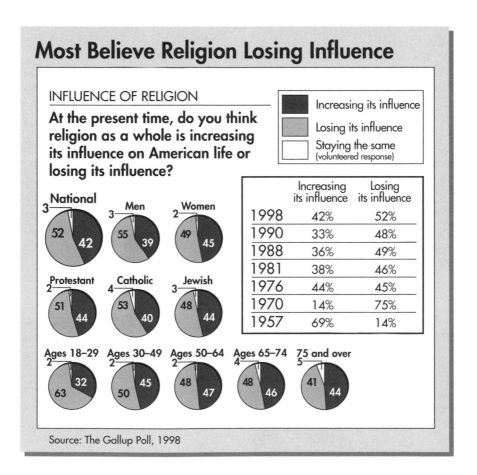

Most Believe Religion Losing Influence

INFLUENCE OF RELIGION

At the present time, do you think religion as a whole is increasing its influence on American life or losing its influence?

- ■ Increasing its influence
- ▨ Losing its influence
- □ Staying the same (volunteered response)

National 3 / 52 / 42
Men 3 / 55 / 39
Women 2 / 49 / 45

Protestant 2 / 51 / 44
Catholic 4 / 53 / 40
Jewish 3 / 48 / 44

Ages 18–29 2 / 32 / 63
Ages 30–49 2 / 45 / 50
Ages 50–64 2 / 48 / 47
Ages 65–74 4 / 48 / 46
75 and over 5 / 41 / 44

	Increasing its influence	Losing its influence
1998	42%	52%
1990	33%	48%
1988	36%	49%
1981	38%	46%
1976	44%	45%
1970	14%	75%
1957	69%	14%

Source: The Gallup Poll, 1998

belief in religion's expanding influence peaked during the 1980s with nearly one-half of the population (49%) affirming its increasing influence in 1985. By the beginning of the 1990s, however, less than one in three (27%) held such a belief. Gradually during the 1990s, more Americans endorsed this notion, and in 1998 42% of the country thought that religion was, once again, increasing in influence.

A dramatic change in public opinion surfaced during the 1960s. Fourteen percent of the populace thought that religion was losing its influence in 1957. Twelve years later, only 14% believed that religion was increasing its influence on American life. 1957 was the year in which the largest number of Americans, in forty years of Gallup research, believed in religion's expanding influence. Moreover, 1969 saw the lowest level of support for religion's increase in public influence. This represents a striking shift in conclusions within a very short span of time.

Although support for religion's widening influence is up within recent years, the majority of Americans (52%), nevertheless, believe that religion is losing its influence on society. Across various faith groups, around one-half of the members think that religion is becoming less influential: 51% of Protestants, 53% of Catholics, and 48% of Jews. Among Americans who regard religion as very important to their own lives, 49% conclude that religion is flagging in its power and sway within the modern culture. Forty-eight percent of U.S. adults with postgraduate education hold this conviction as well as 50% of college-educated adults. Among those with no college education, 53% say that religion is losing its influence.

Older Americans' opinions differ from the national trends. A slight plurality of adults (44%) over age 75 suggests that religion's influence is expanding within American public life. Women over age 55 believe the same with even greater conviction. Fifty-one percent of them believe that religion is spreading its influence within the present context.

CHURCH MEMBERSHIP

According to a recent Gallup Poll, nearly seven in ten Americans (69%) are members of a church or synagogue. This statistic has remained relatively stable from the mid-1960s through the 1990s, fluctuating between 65% and 71%. The positive response to this Gallup Poll, which has been asked for over sixty years, peaked in 1947, when 76% of the population claimed membership in some house of worship. Attendance in worship fell to its lowest points in 1996 and 1988; during those years 65% of the nation were members of a church or synagogue.

While the statistics have remained relatively constant since 1939, certain subcategories of the American population are more inclined to affiliate with religious bodies. For example, an older Black woman living in the rural South is far more likely to belong to a church than a young White male living in a large city on the West Coast. The two things that most often determine whether or not you are a church member are where you live and how old you are. Six adults in ten (61%) in the under-30 age bracket are members of a church or synagogue, and affiliation increases steadily as people age until it peaks at 81% among those between 65 and 74 years old. Over three in four Southerners (76%) claim membership, compared to just barely over half of those living in the West (56%). Almost three persons in four in rural areas are members (72%) compared to 64% of adults living in cities and metropolitan areas.

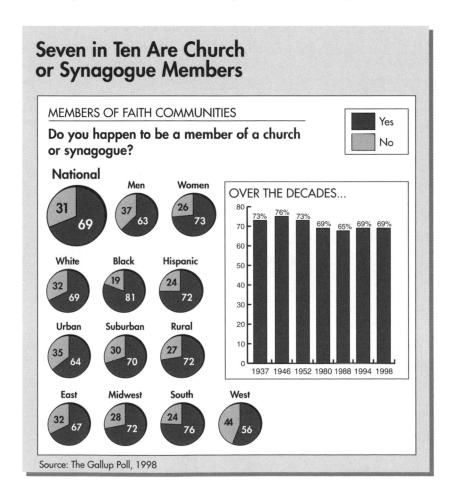

Seven in Ten Are Church or Synagogue Members

MEMBERS OF FAITH COMMUNITIES

Do you happen to be a member of a church or synagogue?

Yes   No

National 31 / 69
Men 37 / 63
Women 26 / 73

OVER THE DECADES...

1937: 73% 1946: 76% 1952: 73% 1980: 69% 1988: 65% 1994: 69% 1998: 69%

White 32 / 69
Black 19 / 81
Hispanic 24 / 72

Urban 35 / 64
Suburban 30 / 70
Rural 27 / 72

East 32 / 67
Midwest 28 / 72
South 24 / 76
West 44 / 56

Source: The Gallup Poll, 1998

In 1998, as in past years, a higher percentage of women than men report being church members. Eighty-two percent of women over the age of 55 belong to a place of worship; only 56% of men under 30 claim the same. Blacks are more likely than Hispanics and Whites to be church members (81% of Blacks compared to 72% of Hispanics and 69% of Whites).

It is important to understand that membership, as measured by Gallup surveys, is a state of mind that may or may not reflect official denominational determinations for counting church members. It should also be noted that adherents of certain churches—for example, the Roman Catholic and Eastern Orthodox—are considered members at birth. Undoubtedly, many local pastors, rabbis, and other spiritual leaders would be surprised in some instances by both those who would consider themselves members and those who do not. Gallup reports religious preferences because decades of research have shown that even non-church members in the United States hold membership preferences. Most Americans who are not current church members either have been in the past or will be in the future. These types of surveys are beneficial because they point out overall trends in religious affiliation and reflect the general public's inclinations with regard to church membership and attendance.

CHURCH ATTENDANCE

In a typical week during 1998, two in five adults (40%) attended church or synagogue, a figure that has remained remarkably constant since the early 1960s. The record high points in church attendance occurred during the 1950s. In both 1955 and 1958, almost half of the population (49%) reported attending church or synagogue within the past week. The trend reached its nadir of 37% in 1940, as the Depression neared its end prior to U.S. involvement in World War II.

Attendance is strongest among residents of the South (48%). Midwesterners fall behind Southerners as well as the national average with 38% of adults attending church within the past seven days. In the East, attendance drops to 40% of the population while less than one in three in the West (32%) goes to church during the typical week.

Blacks and Hispanics exceed White Americans in church attendance. Fifty-five percent of Blacks and 48% of Hispanics are likely to attend church within the past week; only 39% of Whites hold similar inclinations.

Attendance is highly influenced by age, with just 33% of the nation's young adults (ages 18–29) going to church, compared to 52% of senior adults (ages 65–74). This tendency could have great impact upon future attendance as members of the population bulge known as the Baby Boomers begin to reach age 50 and beyond. If past patterns hold true, it may become tougher and tougher to find a seat in the pews.

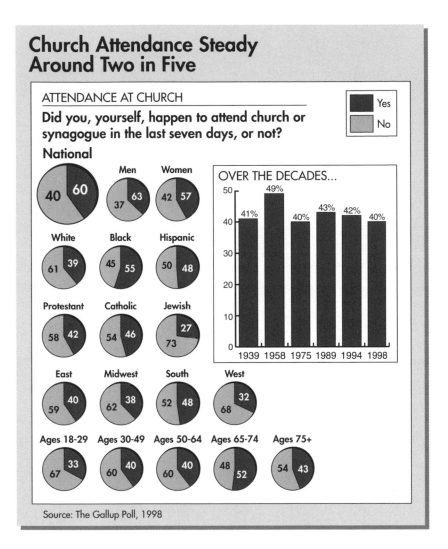

Church Attendance Steady Around Two in Five

ATTENDANCE AT CHURCH

Did you, yourself, happen to attend church or synagogue in the last seven days, or not?

■ Yes
□ No

National

40 | 60

Men
37 | 63

Women
42 | 57

White
61 | 39

Black
45 | 55

Hispanic
50 | 48

Protestant
58 | 42

Catholic
54 | 46

Jewish
73 | 27

OVER THE DECADES...

1939 — 41%
1958 — 49%
1975 — 40%
1989 — 43%
1994 — 42%
1998 — 40%

East
59 | 40

Midwest
62 | 38

South
52 | 48

West
68 | 32

Ages 18-29
67 | 33

Ages 30-49
60 | 40

Ages 50-64
60 | 40

Ages 65-74
48 | 52

Ages 75+
54 | 43

Source: The Gallup Poll, 1998

Catholics outshine Protestants and Jews in church attendance. In 1998, 46% of Catholics in this country reported church attendance within the past week. Protestants fell slightly behind with 42% attending during the week. Jews, on the other hand, lagged far behind with 27% attending a synagogue service during the past week.

RELIGIOUS PREFERENCE

People in this country usually express a religious preference, and for the great majority that preference is the Christian faith, according to a half century of

Little Change in Religious Preferences

RELIGIOUS PREFERENCE

What is your religious preference—Protestant, Roman Catholic, Jewish, or an Orthodox religion such as the Greek or Russian Orthodox Church?

	Protestant	Catholic	Orthodox	Mormon	Jewish	Muslim	Hindu	None
National	59%	27%	1%	1%	1%	—	—	6%
Male	56	27	2	1	1	—	—	7
Female	60	27	1	1	1	—	—	4
White	57	29	1	1	2	—	—	5
Non-White	70	14	2	—	1	1	—	6
Black	81	9	3	—	1	—	—	2
Hispanic	33	50	3	2	—	—	—	5
East	46	40	1	1	2	—	—	6
Midwest	57	29	1	—	1	—	—	5
South	72	17	1	1	1	—	—	4
West	53	24	2	2	2	—	—	9
Postgraduate	55	24	2	—	4	1	—	8
College	54	29	1	1	2	—	—	7
No College	64	24	1	1	1	—	—	4

	Protestant	Catholic	Jewish	Other	None
1998	59%	27%	1%	7%	6%
1994	60	24	2	8	6
1990	56	25	2	6	11
1986	58	27	2	4	9
1981	59	28	2	4	7
1974	60	27	2	5	6
1967	67	25	3	3	2
1947	69	20	5	1	6

Source: The Gallup Poll, 1998   — = less than 1%

Gallup research. Since 1972, about six in ten Americans have claimed Protestantism as their religious preference. Prior to the 1970s, that figure was even higher. In 1962, seven in ten Americans were Protestants. The percentage tumbled during the 1960s, a turbulent decade for all religious groups in this country. Since then, the level of affiliation has remained fairly constant, around the 60-percent mark.

Just over one person in four (27%) embraces the Roman Catholic faith. The Orthodox, Mormon, and Jewish faiths each claim an additional 1% of the general population. Muslims and Hindus comprise less than 1% each, although certain sections of the population ascribe to these faiths with more frequency. For example, 1% of non-Whites in America claim to be Muslims, practicing the faith of Islam. Furthermore, among non-Whites with postgraduate education, 4% choose Muslim and an additional 2% select Hindu as their religious preference.

In 1998, the South is a Protestant stronghold, as it has been for decades. Seventy-two percent of Southerners name one of the Protestant denominations as their preference. Protestants also predominate in the Midwest (57%), but their presence is somewhat lighter in the West (53%) and the East (46%).

Catholics are most numerous in the East, where they account for two in five adults (40%). Nearly one person in four is Roman Catholic in the Midwest and the West (29% and 24%, respectively), but there are fewer Catholics in the South (17%). People living in the West subscribe the least to any particular religious faith. Nearly one in ten Westerners (9%) claims no religious preference at all, which is more than double the statistic found in the South.

Preference for Protestantism increases as people grow older. Under age 30, 50% of the population name it as their religious preference, but by age 50 the proportion preferring a Protestant denomination swells to 65%. The trend continues so that nearly three in four Americans over age 75 (73%) prefer Protestant expressions of faith over all others. The reverse pattern is true for Roman Catholics, with 29% of those under age 30 naming it as their preference, but by age 75, just 19% still hold to the Catholic faith.

The religious preferences of Whites closely mirror the national averages, but Blacks are much more likely to prefer a Protestant denomination (81%) than to be Catholics (9%), Orthodox (3%), or Jews (1%).

It is important to understand that statements of religious preference may not always match statistics on religious membership because of differences in the way individual faiths and denominations may determine membership. The Gallup survey measures individual religious preference, which is a much looser means of measuring religious association.

DENOMINATIONAL AFFILIATION

The percentages of adults in the 1990s who state a preference for mainline Protestant denominations continue to fall below the levels recorded in the 1960s and early and mid-1970s. In the 1998 audit, 18% of Americans claimed to be members of some type of Baptist church, 9% Methodist, 5% Lutheran, and 4% Pentecostal or Church of God. People who preferred Presbyterian churches, Church of Christ, as well as nondenominational churches each comprised 3% of the population. Another 2% chose Episcopalianism, and a remaining 7% selected some other Protestant denomination. One must remember that these figures reflect Americans' preference for, and not necessarily their membership in, a specific denomination of religious faith.

Statistics of declining church rolls within recent years mirror the shrinking percentages of Americans who in 1998 selected one of the Protestant denominations for their religious preference. In 1967, for instance, 14% of the country preferred the Methodist denomination. Three decades later, that figure fell to just 9% of the population. In another case, 6% of Americans in 1967 affiliated with the Presbyterian church; in 1998 only 3% picked the same denomination as their preference.

Baptists, who include both "mainline" and evangelical churches, have a long-standing tradition as the largest religious group in the United States.

Mainline Affiliation Dwindles

AFFILIATION
What is your denominational preference?

	Southern Baptist	Other Baptist	Methodist	Presbyterian	Episcopalian	Lutheran	Pentecostal Assy of God	Church of Christ	Non-denominational	Other
National	8%	10%	9%	3%	2%	5%	4%	3%	3%	7%
Male	7	10	9	3	1	5	3	3	4	6
Female	9	11	9	4	2	6	4	2	2	8
White	7	8	9	4	2	6	4	3	3	7
Black	17	30	9	1	—	—	4	2	5	8
Hispanic	7	3	2	—	—	1	9	—	1	1
East	3	7	10	3	2	3	2	1	2	8
Midwest	5	9	9	3	—	12	3	3	3	8
South	17	16	11	4	2	3	5	3	3	4
West	6	6	3	3	2	4	4	3	6	9
1997	8	11	9	4	2	6	3	3	3	6
1996	8	10	9	4	2	6	3	2	4	8
1995	10	9	9	4	2	6	3	2	3	9
1994	10	10	10	4	2	7	3	2	4	8
1993	10	10	10	3	2	6	2	1	3	10
1992	9	10	10	5	2	7	1	—	1	11

SUMMARIES FROM PREVIOUS SURVEYS

	Baptist	Methodist	Lutheran	Presbyterian	Episcopalian
1988	20%	10%	6%	4%	2%
1986	20	9	5	2	2
1984	20	9	7	2	3
1979	19	11	6	4	2
1975	20	11	7	5	3
1967	21	14	7	6	3

Source: The Gallup Poll, 1998   — = less than 1%

Gallup statistics include many different strands of Baptists, including American Baptists, National Baptists, Southern Baptists, and others. The Southern Baptist Convention is the nation's largest Protestant body with over 15 million members throughout the country. Today 8% of the country prefers Southern Baptist churches; additionally, 10% of the populace claims some other Baptist denomination.

Related Gallup studies within recent years show a growing trend among American Protestants—denominational switching. As their beliefs and situations change, many among the religious faithful switch denominations at some point in time. About one adult in four (23%) has moved from the religious group in which he was raised at least once. For the most part, these changes have benefited the Protestant denominations. Among those who have changed denominations, there are nine times as many who are now Protestants (81%) as who have become Catholics (9%). The smaller, splintered Protestant denominations frequently are the beneficiaries of these switches in denominational allegiance.

INFLUENCE OF RELIGION

Although most Americans believe that religion is losing its influence in today's culture, a majority of people in this country continue to think that religion can answer most of today's problems. In 1957, eight in ten U.S. adults (81%) expressed confidence that religion could address contemporary problems and struggles. That very high level of confidence has never been matched in the intervening years, but a majority of the population continue to sustain their faith in the ability of religion to answer problems.

Forty years later, almost two adults in three (65%) believe that religion can answer today's problems. Women are slightly more inclined to endorse this notion than men by a margin of 69% to 60%. Greater disparity surfaces when comparing the opinions of people from different races. A vast majority (84%) of Blacks in the United States think that religion holds the answers to contemporary dilemmas and difficulties. Hispanics also rise above the national average with 69% of them affirming religion's relevance for today's issues and concerns. Whites, on the other hand, dip slightly below national figures with 63% supporting religion's ability to answer current predicaments and questions. Although subcategories of the general population based on age usually reveal striking differences of opinion on matters of religious faith, it appears that the nation's young and senior adults do not differ too much on the issue of religion's relevance. Only four percentage points separate these two groups on this survey. Instead, Gallup research shows more variance in responses based upon individuals' region of the country. Three in four Southerners (75%), for instance, think that religion can answer the problems of today. This contrasts with the opinions of people living in the West, where only 60% of adults hold similar convictions, or the East Coast, where only 57% believe the same.

Protestants are much more apt to regard religion as relevant for tackling today's problems than Roman Catholics or Jews. While 74% of Protestants consider religion germane to contemporary life, only 58% of Catholics and 13% of Jews believe similarly. When surveying the opinions of Americans who do not consider religion important to their personal lives, Gallup uncovered some interesting results. For example, 15% of those who claim religion is "not very important" to their own lives still believe that religion can address and answer all or most of today's problems.

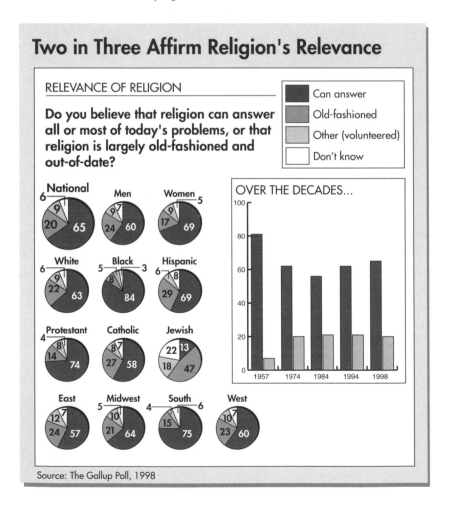

Two in Three Affirm Religion's Relevance

RELEVANCE OF RELIGION

Do you believe that religion can answer all or most of today's problems, or that religion is largely old-fashioned and out-of-date?

- ■ Can answer
- ▨ Old-fashioned
- ▤ Other (volunteered)
- □ Don't know

National: 6, 9, 20, 65
Men: 7, 9, 24, 60
Women: 5, 9, 17, 69

White: 6, 9, 22, 63
Black: 5, 8, 3, 84
Hispanic: 6, 8, 29, 69

Protestant: 4, 8, 14, 74
Catholic: 8, 7, 27, 58
Jewish: 22, 13, 18, 47

East: 12, 7, 24, 57
Midwest: 5, 10, 21, 64
South: 4, 15, 6, 75
West: 10, 7, 23, 60

OVER THE DECADES...

(Bar chart, 1957, 1974, 1984, 1994, 1998)

Source: The Gallup Poll, 1998

Religion and Beliefs

America is a nation of believers. Within the pluralistic milieu of religious ideologies, people of this country resoundingly affirm a belief in God, miracles, and life after death. The globalization of American culture delivers foreign religions and spiritual practices to the doorsteps of many U.S. households. As a result, Eastern notions such as reincarnation gain increasing acceptance every year among adults in this nation. The religious landscape of the United States contains legion religious groups and sects. Agreement within this potpourri of faiths and dogmas seems out of reach, but Americans appear to be united in their commitment, at least to believe in something.

Ninety-five percent of adults believe in God or a universal spirit. In keeping with the trend over the last half century, only one in twenty adults could be described as holding an atheistic or agnostic position. Despite the twentieth century's sweeping changes in American culture and social structure, Americans maintain consistent beliefs within the religious domain. Americans demonstrate openness to the prospect of miracles, the afterlife, heaven, hell, and angels. The majority hesitate, however, to endorse religious beliefs such as biblical inerrancy and creation without evolution.

Two in three adults expect to exist in some form following death. The overwhelming majority of these surmise this existence will be a positive expe rience, and most of them also employ the metaphor of a journey in their understanding of the afterlife. More Americans believe in heaven than in hell, although a majority of adults affirm the existence of both places. A strong majority of people (84%) link a person's actions on earth to the quality of his or her afterlife. Seventy-eight percent of the country links people's spiritual state at the time of death to their life after death. Nearly seven in ten Americans (69%) believe a spiritual awakening influences their existence in the afterlife.

Most Americans embrace a Judeo-Christian religious identity, and, consequently, a large majority of U.S. adults (80%) regard the Bible as inspired Scripture. Only 17% of the population regard the Bible as a book of fables, legends, history, and moral precepts. Belief in the Bible's inspiration and authority has remained at a high level for nearly fifty years. Americans seem to marginalize the academy's critical discussion of the Bible's authority and fallibility when it comes to basic understanding of Scripture. However, fewer adults today maintain a fundamentalist interpretation that advances a literal reading of the Bible. For example, in 1963, 65% of adults considered the Bible to be literally true. Thirty-five years later, the figure has halved to its current level of belief (33%).

The modern era's proliferation of scientific hypotheses and theories has not caused believing Americans to reexamine their religious convictions. The concerns expressed by many religious advocates in the Tennessee trial of John Scopes for teaching evolutionary theory to high school students have not materialized nearly to the degree that they once feared. Jefferson's "wall of separation" between church and state has caused evolutionary notions to take precedence in American classrooms without the inclusion of a creationist interpretation. This has not, however, really altered Americans' understanding of human beginnings over the past several decades. Only one in ten people (10%) today, for instance, supports an evolutionary theory that excludes God. In fact, the plurality of respondents believe God created humans pretty much in their present form at one time within the last ten thousand years. The second most popular response involves an evolutionary understanding of human development under the guidance and providence of God. A smaller group of Americans endorses evolution without divine influence. In sum, the dominant American belief on human beginnings is evolution with God's involvement in the process.

Evangelism in the United States dates back to the first and second Great Awakenings of early American history. The Evangelical movement of the late twentieth century traces some of its roots to neo-Orthodoxy, the theological renewal of this century inspired by the writings of German theologian Karl Barth. Stressing the authority of biblical witness and revived scriptural understandings on the Trinity, redemption, grace, and ecclesiology, neo-Orthodoxy wrestled traditional Christian doctrines away from the enlightened, liberal idealism that prevailed in the eighteenth and nineteenth centuries. Recently, the revivalism of ministers such as Dr. Billy Graham has fanned the evangelical flames across denominational boundaries. Many observers of American religion have centered their attention upon the beliefs of contemporary evangelicals.

As we approach the end of the twentieth century, distinctions can be drawn between evangelicals and non-evangelicals on numerous lifestyle matters. Take, for instance, the consumption of alcohol. While seven in ten non-evangelicals drink alcohol on a regular basis, only one in four evangelicals claim the same practice. More evangelical believers eschew smoking and gambling than those in the general population of this country. Distinctions become blurred on paranormal and supernatural matters. The differences between evangelicals and the rest of the country on beliefs in reincarnation, ghosts, and astrology are statistically miniscule. Curiously, evangelical adherents are twice as likely as the general population to affirm belief in channeling which allows a spirit-being to temporarily assume control of a human being during a trance. While this does not suggest greater participation of evangelicals in these practices, some have suggested that it does underscore the evangelicals' greater inclination toward beliefs in the supernatural.

The United States is brimming with religious adherents who embrace myriad religious faiths. The spiritual frontier for this country has expanded and incorporated diverse foreign ideologies and philosophies throughout the twentieth century. The trend of the last fifty years shows a commitment among the American people to embrace religious convictions. As more of the international community becomes linked with American communities and neighborhoods, the options for those religious convictions will become even more manifold than they are today. Ours is an era of customization. From custom-designed homes to individually arranged payment options, we are consumers who demand choices and freedom. Americans demonstrate affinities to numerous spiritual beliefs and tenets. People in the United States favor a faith that meets personal needs and answers individual concerns. The religious liberty most Americans cherish and celebrate has enabled religion in this country to flourish in many forms and to become a profound molder of the American character.

Belief in God

Almost two-thirds of Americans confidently affirm God's existence. Ninety-five percent of the American public believes in God or what they term a "Higher Power." A comparison of the religious climate in the 1990s with that of nearly fifty years ago reveals an overall consistency in convictions about God or a divine power. Despite numerous challenges by some members of the clergy and social observers that America is moving toward being an atheistic nation, the American people continue to confirm a belief in God. Evidence does suggest, however, that the percentage of people with a deep, lived-out faith is much smaller than the overall percentages on religious belief would seem to suggest. Over the past fifty years of research, the percentage of Americans who believe in God has never dropped below 90%. In 1947 *Ladies' Home Journal* reported on the religious beliefs, practices, as well as relationship between religious belief and ethical practice in an article titled, "God and the American People" by Lincoln Barnett. On the basis of the survey findings, Barnett wrote:

> It is evident that a profound gulf lies between America's avowed ethical standards and the observable realities of national life. What may be more alarming is the gap between what Americans *think* they do and what they *do* do.[3]

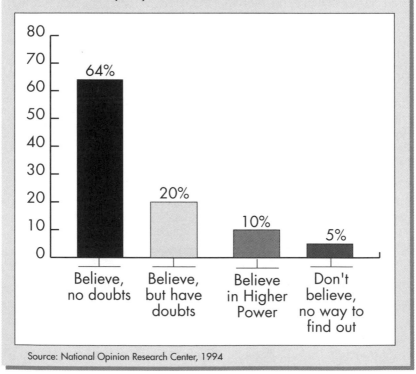

Americans' Belief in God Remains Strong for Fifty Years

Please tell me which statement come closest to expressing what you believe about God. I know that God really exists, and I have no doubts about it; While I have doubts, I feel that I do believe in God; I find myself believing in God some of the time, but not at others; I don't believe in a personal God, but I do believe in a Higher Power of some kind; I don't know whether there is a god, and I don't believe there is any way to find out; I don't believe in God.

Source: National Opinion Research Center, 1994

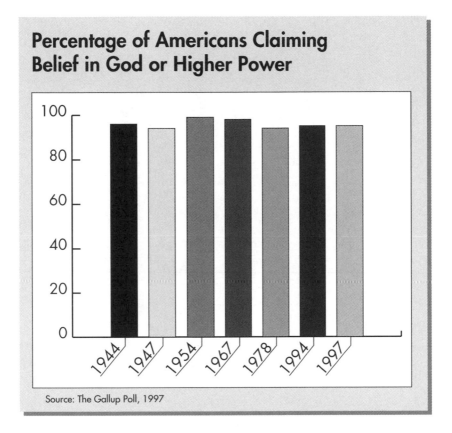

Percentage of Americans Claiming Belief in God or Higher Power

Source: The Gallup Poll, 1997

Three luminaries in the theological world analyzed the findings; each theologian represented one of the three major faiths—Protestantism, Judaism, and Catholicism—namely, Reinhold Niebuhr, Simon Greenberg, and George B. Ford. Commenting on the presence of breadth but the lack of depth in religious belief, Dr. Greenberg wrote, "While the mind that enters a university may be ready for adult fare in the secular field, all it gets in the religious field is infant food."[4] Current Gallup data would suggest that Dr. Greenberg's comment would apply to contemporary America, as well.

MIRACLES

The Enlightenment's reliance upon empirical, rational phenomena has heavily influenced contemporary culture. Surprisingly, however, an overwhelming majority of Americans believe in miracles (79%). Americans appear to disregard their propensity to rely solely upon rational knowledge when considering the possibility that miracles occur. Religion shapes the opinions of Americans regarding miracles: believers are more than twice as likely to believe in them than those who regard religion as "not very important" in their lives. Similarly, those who attend church on a weekly basis are more likely to believe in miracles than those who attend monthly, seldom, or never. Most interesting, only 4% of weekly church attenders do not believe in miracles— a striking comparison with those who seldom or never attend church (20%).

Education also conditions a person's view of miracles. On the whole, the more education one receives, the less likely he or she is to affirm the existence of miracles. Americans with postgraduate education are twice as likely not to believe in miracles compared with those with no college education at all. Nonetheless, an overwhelming majority of people (79%)—regardless of their level of education—believe in miracles.

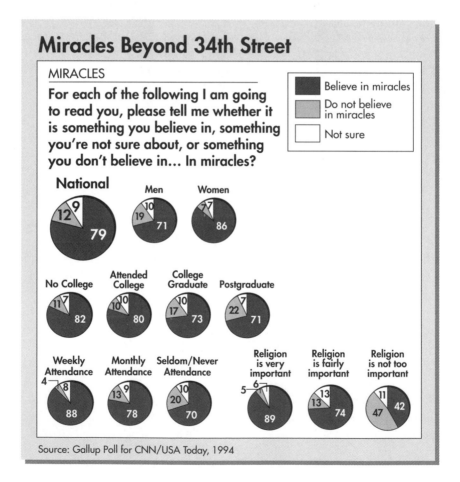

Miracles Beyond 34th Street

MIRACLES

For each of the following I am going to read you, please tell me whether it is something you believe in, something you're not sure about, or something you don't believe in... In miracles?

- Believe in miracles
- Do not believe in miracles
- Not sure

National
9
12
79

Men
10
19
71

Women
7
7
86

No College
11 7
82

Attended College
10
10
80

College Graduate
10
17
73

Postgraduate
7
22
71

Weekly Attendance
4
8
88

Monthly Attendance
13 9
78

Seldom/Never Attendance
10
20
70

Religion is very important
5 6
89

Religion is fairly important
13
13
74

Religion is not too important
11
47 42

Source: Gallup Poll for CNN/USA Today, 1994

In a separate survey conducted by Gallup,[5] Americans revealed a difference between belief in miracles and a first-hand experience with the miraculous. While most people in the country continue to affirm belief in miracles, fewer (41%) said that they had "experienced something that might be described as miraculous." Among women, nearly half (47%) experienced some aspect of the miraculous. With men, however, that figure drops to just over one-third (34%). Both belief in and experience with miracles run highest among those who say that religion is "very important" in their lives.

LIFE AFTER DEATH

Regarding life after death, most Americans believe the following:

1. They will exist in some form after death.

2. Heaven exists, but their chances of going there are less than "excellent."

Is there a heaven?

Recent polls indicate that most people believe in heaven. However, doubting the existence of heaven increases as people receive more secular education. Respondents were asked "Do you think there is a heaven where people who have led good lives are eternally rewarded?"

What are your chances of going to heaven?

National figures in percent.

Excellent	29
Good	48
Fair	17
Poor	3

Do you believe in heaven?

National figures in percent.

☐ Yes
▨ No
■ Not sure

	No college	Some college	College graduate	Post graduate
Not sure	5	9		
Yes	94	90	16	21
No			80	75

Source: Gallup Poll for CNN/USA Today, Dec. 1994   Figures shown (+/- 3%).

J. Farnell

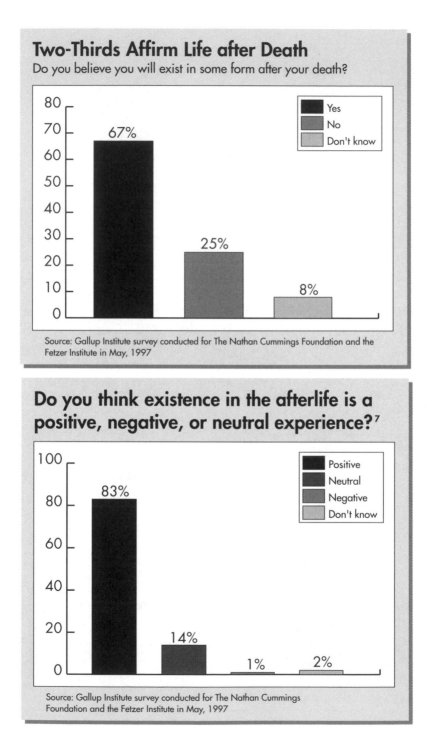

Two-Thirds Affirm Life after Death

Do you believe you will exist in some form after your death?

Legend:
- Yes
- No
- Don't know

67%
25%
8%

Source: Gallup Institute survey conducted for The Nathan Cummings Foundation and the Fetzer Institute in May, 1997

Do you think existence in the afterlife is a positive, negative, or neutral experience?[7]

Legend:
- Positive
- Neutral
- Negative
- Don't know

83%
14%
1%
2%

Source: Gallup Institute survey conducted for The Nathan Cummings Foundation and the Fetzer Institute in May, 1997

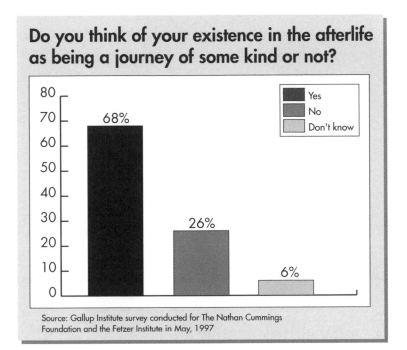

Do you think of your existence in the afterlife as being a journey of some kind or not?

Source: Gallup Institute survey conducted for The Nathan Cummings Foundation and the Fetzer Institute in May, 1997

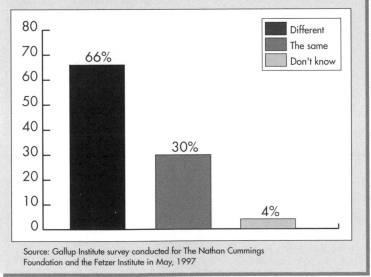

Do you believe that the quality of existence after death is different for different people or the same for all?

Source: Gallup Institute survey conducted for The Nathan Cummings Foundation and the Fetzer Institute in May, 1997

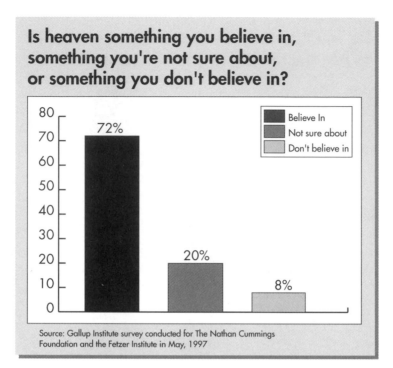

Is heaven something you believe in, something you're not sure about, or something you don't believe in?

Believe In
Not sure about
Don't believe in

72%
20%
8%

Source: Gallup Institute survey conducted for The Nathan Cummings Foundation and the Fetzer Institute in May, 1997

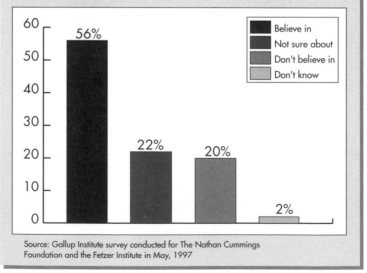

Is hell something you believe in, something you're not sure about, or something you don't believe in?

Believe in
Not sure about
Don't believe in
Don't know

56%
22%
20%
2%

Source: Gallup Institute survey conducted for The Nathan Cummings Foundation and the Fetzer Institute in May, 1997

3. Hell exists, and their chances of going there are "fair" or "poor."

4. There will be some kind of journey in the afterlife.

Even before the age of Egyptian pyramids, people have shown a preoccupation with the afterlife. In the modern era, advances in medicine and technology have enabled individuals to be "brought back to life" after near-death experiences, and these have spurred Americans' interest in the afterlife. Among those Americans who believe they will exist after death in some form, a strong majority believe this existence will be a positive experience, and most (72%) surmise that they will grow spiritually through the process. Many more believe in heaven than believe in hell. In fact, just over half of them (56%) believe in hell.

Opinions differ on those factors that influence one's quality of continued existence after death. The following are the most popular responses and the corresponding percentage of adults who affirm their influence in the afterlife[6]:

Everything you did in your life. 84%

Your spiritual state at the time of your death 78%

Having had a spiritual awakening or decision. 69%

Rituals that take place at the time of your death. 23%

Rituals that take place after your death 20%

No opinion/No answer. 4%

Some surprising demographic patterns emerge in attitudes concerning life after death. Older Americans and those adults with lower incomes hold the most traditional religious views regarding the afterlife. Seventy-two percent of college graduates, 69% of those with some college education, and 63% of those with a high school degree or less believe in an afterlife. Americans inconsistently maintain views on the afterlife. For example, 72% of those who believe in some form of an afterlife affirm the existence of heaven, but only

56% of them believe in hell. Most people who believe in an afterlife think it will be a positive experience (83%).

REINCARNATION

A sizable majority of the American public believes in reincarnation, undoubtedly influenced in considerable measure by the rising popularity of Eastern religions among mainstream Americans. Reincarnation suggests that the soul or spirit may go on to inhabit other bodies in successive lives here on earth before eventually moving on to either heaven or hell. While the number of adults who reject reincarnation continues to represent a majority of Americans (53% do

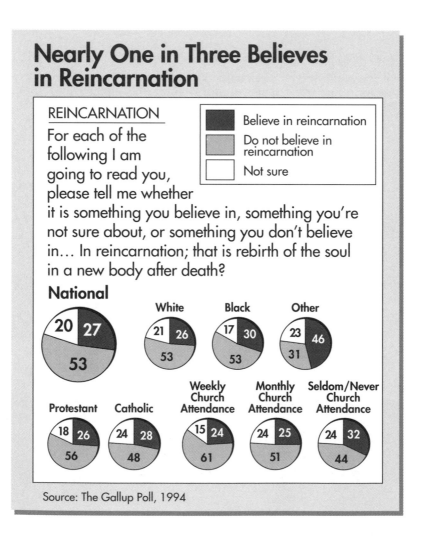

Nearly One in Three Believes in Reincarnation

REINCARNATION

For each of the following I am going to read you, please tell me whether it is something you believe in, something you're not sure about, or something you don't believe in… In reincarnation; that is rebirth of the soul in a new body after death?

- Believe in reincarnation
- Do not believe in reincarnation
- Not sure

National
20 27 53

White
21 26 53

Black
17 30 53

Other
23 46 31

Protestant
18 26 56

Catholic
24 28 48

Weekly Church Attendance
15 24 61

Monthly Church Attendance
24 25 51

Seldom/Never Church Attendance
24 32 44

Source: The Gallup Poll, 1994

not believe in reincarnation), the number of people who do believe continues to grow. In a 1990 study conducted by The Gallup Poll, 21% of adults said they believed in reincarnation. By 1994 that figure had grown to 27%.

Even though Whites and Blacks in this country almost always follow one of the Abrahamic religions, which do not recognize reincarnation, over one in four affirms the rebirth of the soul in a new body on earth after death. In total, 26% of Whites say they believe in reincarnation and an additional 21% say they are not sure about it, while 30% of Blacks support reincarnation and 17% express uncertainty about it. Among those adults belonging to other ethnic groups, the number who say they believe in it jumps to nearly half (46%).

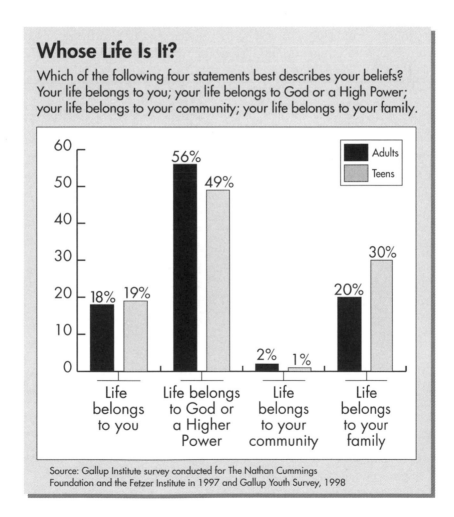

Whose Life Is It?

Which of the following four statements best describes your beliefs? Your life belongs to you; your life belongs to God or a High Power; your life belongs to your community; your life belongs to your family.

Source: Gallup Institute survey conducted for The Nathan Cummings Foundation and the Fetzer Institute in 1997 and Gallup Youth Survey, 1998

Church attendance and religious faith continue to play a dominant role in shaping Americans' beliefs. Those adults who attend church on a weekly basis are less likely to believe in reincarnation. Sixty-one percent of weekly church-goers do not believe in it, but that number decreases to 44% among those adults who attend church seldom or never. Likewise, Protestants demonstrate greater resistance to reincarnation when compared with Catholics. Fifty-six percent of Protestants regard reincarnation as untenable; the number falls to 48% among Catholic believers.

PRIMACY OF GOD

Most Americans believe in God or a Higher Power, but fewer believe this God or Higher Power has absolute primacy in their lives. The percentage who states that their life belongs to God or a Higher Power, nevertheless, exceeds those who choose family, community, or self. This trend proves true for both adults (56%) and teens (49%); however, a difference between adults and teens is evident among those who believe their lives belong to their families. Nearly one-third of American teens believe that their lives belong to their families whereas the percentage tumbles to one-fifth among our nation's adults.

It is interesting to note that among adults, the percentage of people who claim that their lives belong to God is greater than the combined percentages of the public who believe that their lives belong to their families, their communities, or themselves. Although the percentages among teens do not exactly mirror the results among adults, one can clearly see that a plurality of teens view their lives as belonging to God or a Higher Power. It appears that times of death and dying bring to the surface the sharpest distinction between those who believe their life is God's and those who believe their lives belong to themselves, to their family, or to their community. Those Americans who affirm the former are less likely to worry about having completed their "life work," having the chance to say good-bye to someone, dying alone, or experiencing great physical pain near the time of death. These adults are not completely immune to anxiety at times of death. These same Americans, for instance, express more concern about not being forgiven by God, dying when they are "cut off from God," or not having a blessing from a family member or member of the clergy.

BELIEFS ON THE BIBLE

Disagreement abounds on the issue of biblical inerrancy and authority. Throughout the twentieth century theologians, pastors, and members of the laity have disputed the extent to which one can believe the words of Scripture. Gallup studies between 1976 and 1998 show a diversity of opinions on the matter. Yet a general trend on the national level can be discerned. Most Americans consider the Bible to be a collection of inspired writings, but "not everything in it should be taken literally." This trend is mirrored among Whites (49% agreeing with the second statement), adults with postgraduate schooling (56%), and college graduates (58%).

Differences of opinion, however, do exist. Consider, for example, the striking contrast in comparing the responses of Blacks and Whites. A majority of Blacks (54%) believe that the Bible is the "actual word of God and is to be

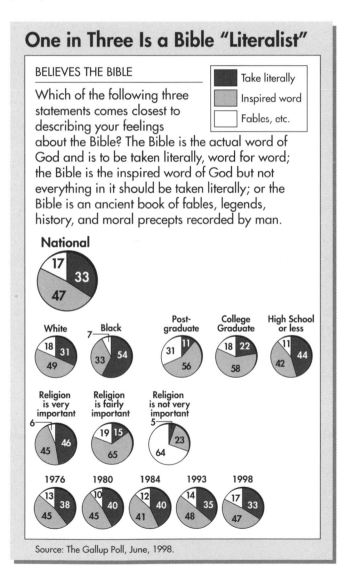

One in Three Is a Bible "Literalist"

BELIEVES THE BIBLE

Which of the following three statements comes closest to describing your feelings about the Bible? The Bible is the actual word of God and is to be taken literally, word for word; the Bible is the inspired word of God but not everything in it should be taken literally; or the Bible is an ancient book of fables, legends, history, and moral precepts recorded by man.

■ Take literally
▨ Inspired word
□ Fables, etc.

Source: The Gallup Poll, June, 1998.

taken literally, word for word," but only 31% of Whites feel the same. In addition, women are more likely than men to affirm this interpretation of the Bible (37% of women versus 30% of men).

Americans with postgraduate education are nearly three times more likely to view the Bible as a book of fables, legends, history, and moral precepts recorded by humans than to believe it should be taken literally. Those who claim that religion is "not very important" in their lives disagree the most with literal interpretations of the Bible. These Americans are, remarkably, twelve times more likely to believe that the Bible is a book of fables, legends, history, and moral precepts than they are to believe that the Bible is the actual word of God to be taken literally and as inerrant. More Americans are moving toward an interpretation of the Bible as a book of fables, history, and moral precepts. Although this still constitutes only a small percentage of the general population, the percentages have gradually increased since 1980. Attempts at demythologizing the Bible that have been ongoing in the academy for years seem to be moving more and more from the classroom to the pews.

In the 1980s Americans were more likely to regard the Bible as the actual word of God compared with opinions in the 1990s. Similarly, the 1980s is the decade in which Americans were least likely to regard it as a collection of fables, legends, history, and moral precepts recorded by man. Since then the public tends to affirm the inspiration of biblical writings but is not as comfortable affirming a literal reading of the texts.

This move toward understanding the Bible as the *inspired*, and not necessarily as the *actual*, word of God is one of the most dramatic shifts in religious beliefs since the 1960s. As recently as 1963, two persons in three viewed the Bible as the actual word of God, to be taken literally, word for word. Today, only one person in three still holds to that interpretation. Instead, most people in 1998 (47%) view the Bible as the inspired word of God.

BELIEFS RELATED TO SCIENCE

The issues of creation versus evolution find their origin with Charles Darwin's text, *On the Origin of the Human Species,* published in 1859. The Scopes Trial of 1925 exacerbated the controversy and brought the debate regarding human beginnings to the forefront of public discourse. These matters have an ongoing influence in contemporary society in arenas such as public education and bioethics. Human cloning and other ethical dilemmas in the medical sector continue to bring this historic debate into the public dialogue.

1997 Gallup studies affirm trends that appeared fifteen years earlier. Most Americans (44%) believe that God created human beings pretty much in their

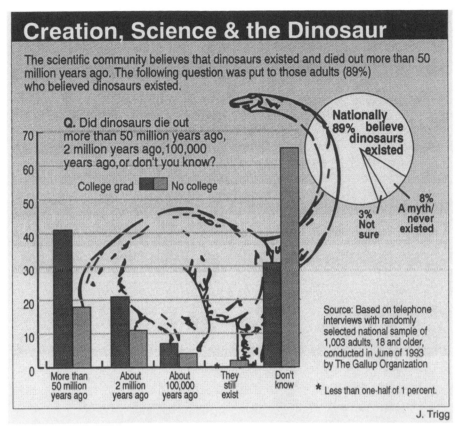

Creation, Science & the Dinosaur

The scientific community believes that dinosaurs existed and died out more than 50 million years ago. The following question was put to those adults (89%) who believed dinosaurs existed.

Q. Did dinosaurs die out more than 50 million years ago, 2 million years ago, 100,000 years ago, or don't you know?

College grad ■ ■ No college

Nationally 89% believe dinosaurs existed

8% A myth/never existed

3% Not sure

More than 50 million years ago | About 2 million years ago | About 100,000 years ago | They still exist | Don't know

Source: Based on telephone interviews with randomly selected national sample of 1,003 adults, 18 and older, conducted in June of 1993 by The Gallup Organization

* Less than one-half of 1 percent.

J. Trigg

present form at one time within the last ten thousand years or so. Among those adults who do not hold the so-called "creationism" interpretation of human origins, an overwhelming majority believes that God guided the evolutionary process. Only a minute percentage of Americans (10%) affirm evolution without God's participation.

Men are almost equally as likely to support creationism as they are to endorse evolution with God's participation. By contrast, women show a clear inclination to embrace creationism over evolution. Likewise, Protestants (52%) are more likely to believe in a creationist interpretation of human origins than Roman Catholics (39%). Pope John Paul II recently stated that evolutionary theory is not incompatible with religious faith, and many Roman Catholics in the United States demonstrated a predisposition to welcome the Pope's message.[8] Roman Catholics in this country depart from the national norm on this issue; most Catholics believe that human beings have evolved in a process under God's direction.

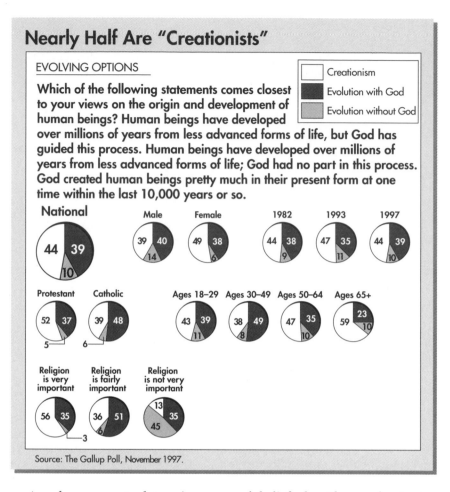

Nearly Half Are "Creationists"

EVOLVING OPTIONS

□ Creationism
■ Evolution with God
▨ Evolution without God

Which of the following statements comes closest to your views on the origin and development of human beings? Human beings have developed over millions of years from less advanced forms of life, but God has guided this process. Human beings have developed over millions of years from less advanced forms of life; God had no part in this process. God created human beings pretty much in their present form at one time within the last 10,000 years or so.

Source: The Gallup Poll, November 1997.

Age also appears to determine a person's beliefs about human beginnings. Older Americans are much more likely to embrace a strict creationist interpretation than their youthful counterparts (59% compared with 43%). Young and middle-age adults (ages 30 to 49) break from the national norm and endorse a theory that integrates God into the process of human evolution. The only subcategory of the American public that tends to favor an evolutionary interpretation that does not involve God is that sector of the population that regards religion as "not very important."

Just over one-third of the American population (38%) believe in extraterrestrial life. Between 1970 and 1990, the figures hovered around the 50% mark, but research conducted in 1996 suggests that Americans' level of belief in life on other planets is returning to the lower levels of belief prominent during the

1960s. A striking percentage of the populace remains undecided on this matter. At times, one out of every five adults expresses uncertainty on the issue of extraterrestrial life; 1996 data show that 18% are "not sure" about the prospect of people like ourselves living on other planets. Although slight fluctuations have occurred, this number has maintained consistently near the 20% mark for the past three decades.

Extraterrestrial Life Stumps Americans

EXTRATERRESTRIAL LIFE

Do you think there are people somewhat like ourselves living on other planets in the universe or not?

	Yes	No	No Opinion
1996	38%	44%	18%
1990	46%	36%	18%
1989	41%	48%	11%
1987	50%	34%	16%
1978	51%	33%	16%
1973	46%	38%	16%
1966	34%	46%	20%

Source: The Gallup Poll, 1996

	Yes	No	
National	38%	44%	18%
Male	46%	38%	16%
Female	31%	50%	19%
Protestant	31%	49%	20%
Catholic	50%	41%	9%
Religion very important	35%	47%	18%
Religion fairly important	39%	43%	18%
Religion not very important	53%	33%	14%

Source: The Gallup Poll, September, 1996

Fifteen percentage points separate men and women on the topic of extraterrestrial life; men are more likely than women to believe in extraterrestrial life (46% compared with 31%). One out of two Roman Catholics thinks that there are people living on other planets; only 31% of Protestants conclude the same. Gallup research also showed that 48% of adults who described themselves as "very" or "somewhat superstitious" subscribe to belief in extraterrestrial life. In contrast, of those who describe themselves as "not at all superstitious," only 28% reason that there are people living on other planets.

The importance of religion in one's life influences people's convictions to some degree. Among those Americans who claim that religion is "very important" to them, just over one-third believe in extraterrestrial life (35%). By contrast over one-half (53%) of adults who say that religion is "not very important" think that people like us exist on other planets in the universe.

BELIEFS OF EVANGELICALS

Born-again or evangelical Christians, although more orthodox in their beliefs and more faithful in their churchgoing, differ little from other Americans on a number of non-Christian beliefs such as astrology, reincarnation, ghosts, and channeling. Nearly 40% of the American population is born again, and the pronounced distinctions of their beliefs appear more often when reviewing moral issues. For example, evangelicals are more likely to differ from the general population on matters such as abortion and prayer in schools.

Surprising Beliefs of Evangelicals

Findings from recent Gallup surveys conducted in 1997, 1996, and 1995 reveal the following distinctions between those Americans who claim to be born again and those who do not:

	BORN AGAIN	NOT BORN AGAIN
Percentage who use alcohol	25%	70%
Smoke cigarettes	41%	53%
Drinking a problem in your family	40%	52%
Gambling a problem in your family	36%	51%
Gun in your household	44%	50%
Hold pro-choice stance in the abortion debate	33%	58%
Believe that homosexuality is something a person is born with	29%	65%
Believe in ghosts	28%	31%
Believe in reincarnation	20%	24%
Believe in channeling	17%	9%
Have consulted a fortune teller	16%	17%
Believe in astrology	26%	24%

Source: The Gallup Poll, 1997, 1996, 1995.

Whereas only one in three evangelicals accept the pro-choice position in the abortion debate, over half (58%) of non-evangelicals support the pro-choice assertion. Thirty-six percentage points divide the two groups on the matter of the cause of homosexuality. On matters of personal lifestyle, one finds marked differences between the two groups; for example, the born-again segment is less likely to use alcoholic beverages and tobacco.

However, one sees surprisingly little distinction between the two groups on beliefs in supernatural and paranormal phenomena. In fact, evangelicals are slightly more likely to believe in astrology and in witches. The groups vary little with regards to consulting a fortune-teller or belief in reincarnation or ghosts. Of particular interest, Gallup research reveals that people who claim to be born again are twice as likely as others to believe in the New Age concept of "channeling" (allowing a spirit being to temporarily assume control of a human being during a trance). Only 9% of the non-evangelical population affirm a belief in channeling; 17% of evangelicals support its validity.

Meaning of Life

More Americans find themselves living in an environment of greater isolation and further alienation than ever before. Advances in computer technology have granted independence and autonomy to many adults who are now able to work and communicate with the outside world while remaining home alone. Just as previous generations grappled with humanity's role in an industrialized world, Americans today seek to find the meaning and value of their individual lives.

Gallup research suggests that most people in this country think a great deal about the meaning and significance of their lives. An overwhelming majority of Americans (89%) contemplate the basic meaning and value of their lives often ("a lot" or "a fair amount"). Recent surveys' results have confirmed the "me-first" label of the 1980s, which is often criticized for being a decade of self-centered motives and concerns. In 1985, 58% of the nation claimed to think about their life's basic meaning frequently. A decade later, 69% of the population says the same. A difference of eleven percentage points represents significant change in opinion within those thirteen years. Also, the number of people who think about the value and meaning of their lives "only a little" has shrunk from 13% to 8%.

Young people in this country think about the value of their lives the most. Nearly four out of five adults ages 18 to 29 (78%) often reflect on this issue. By contrast, Americans of retirement age (over 65) think about it the least. Within the general population, college-educated men and adults earning more than $75,000 a year ponder the meaning of their lives the least. Protestants mirror the national trends. Eighty-nine percent of them think about the meaning and value of their lives with frequency. Among Roman Catholics, the statistics are slightly higher; 82% of them contemplate the contributions and meaning of their own lives often.

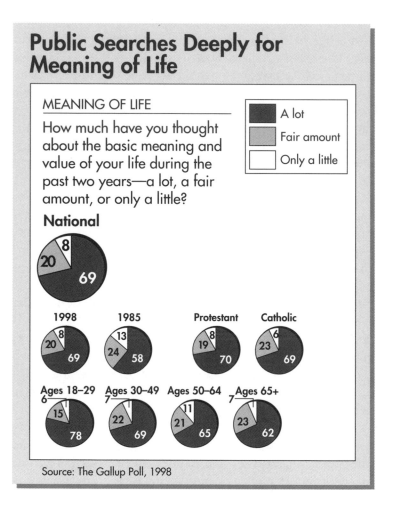

Public Searches Deeply for Meaning of Life

MEANING OF LIFE

How much have you thought about the basic meaning and value of your life during the past two years—a lot, a fair amount, or only a little?

- A lot
- Fair amount
- Only a little

National

Source: The Gallup Poll, 1998

Religion and Practice

Although 95% of Americans claim some religious tenets, a much smaller segment of the population practices their religious faith on a consistent basis. Three prevalent forms of spirituality include prayer, study of Scripture, and charitable acts of service. As Benjamin Franklin once remarked, "Serving God is doing good to man, but praying is thought an easier service and therefore more generally chosen." Indeed, prayer is the spine that holds up all other forms of American spirituality.

Over 90% of Americans today pray, and three in four U.S. adults pray on a daily basis. Most often they pray silently and alone, and nearly one-third of the population always prays before a meal (29%). Common subjects of these prayers involve the well-being of an individual's family, giving thanks, asking for strength or guidance, or asking for forgiveness. Americans also pray for very specific requests such as getting good grades, attaining victory in athletic events, or winning the lottery. Although some might denounce these types of prayers as self-serving or petty, they also reveal the prevailing American notion that prayer is a means by which humans acquire. For most Americans, prayer is petition. Nearly all who pray contend that their petitions have been answered in the past (95%); consequently, a number of Americans trust the power of prayer.

A robust majority of people in this country pray on a daily basis (75%), but only 15% read the Bible with the same frequency. Another 20% of the population read the Bible at least once a week. Most of them (69%) read the Bible alone. Individuals claim that the primary benefit of Scripture reading is that it makes them feel closer to God. Seventy-six percent of the nation says that reading the Bible helps them commune to a greater extent with God. Adults also cite the feeling of peace and finding meaning in life as primary benefits of reading Scripture.

The Chinese characters for "crisis" stand for both "danger" and "opportunity." Many Americans believe times of crisis provide good opportunities for deeper religious growth and spiritual development. Nearly everyone (94%) believes that more time spent in prayer, meditation, or reading the Bible is an effective way to allay personal depression. Almost nine out of ten U.S. adults

(87%) think a pastor or religious leader can offer effective support and encouragement during bouts of depression. Not nearly the same number of people actually pursue these activities during the melancholy seasons of life. For example, the percentage of Americans who seek the help of a pastor during times of discouragement plummets a dramatic sixty points from those who think it would be a good idea (87% think it is a good idea; 27% actually do it). Eight out of ten Americans do find solace in prayer during times of crisis. Women are more inclined to seek spiritual solutions (such as prayer or Bible reading) to crises. Likewise, non-Whites respond to troubles by seeking spiritual solutions much more often than Whites do.

Almost four out of five adults (79%) received some form of religious training as children. An even higher percentage of society's most educated members, individuals with postgraduate education, experienced some form of religious training. Nearly all Americans—regardless of their own experience—would want their children to receive some form of religious instruction. Eighty-nine percent of adults express this desire. Generally, the strongest consensus on this matter arises from the Midwestern and Southern states of the Union. Strong majorities of both Protestants and Catholics wish for some form of religious education for their children.

For many Americans personal piety manifests itself through charitable giving. Gallup research reveals that three-fourths of Americans contributed food, clothing, or other property within the twelve months prior to the survey. Seventy percent contributed monetarily to non-church organizations, and 60% gave money to churches. People are much more willing to contribute material goods than they are to offer their time. Only 42% of the nation reported serving as unpaid volunteer workers for some charity within the last twelve months. Americans clearly prefer to give to charities that benefit the local community—59% compared to 11% benefiting the nation and 12% helping the world.

Involvement in small groups greatly bolsters the likelihood of an individual's practicing his or her personal faith. Princeton University sociologist Robert Wuthnow calls the small group movement in this nation a "quiet revolution."[9] With almost half of the nation's population participating in small groups of some type, many faith communities are employing them as a means to develop greater spiritual disciplines within their congregations. Two members in three of all small groups—not just those that are church-related—say their groups lead them closer to God. For a majority of them (57%), the Bible has become more meaningful to them as a result of their group experience. Many—but not all—church-related small groups center around study of Scriptures and prayer. Wuthnow's landmark study estimates that there are

more than 900,000 Bible study groups and 800,000 adult Sunday school classes in the United States today, and more are beginning every year.

In his 1948 text, *The Shaking of the Foundations*, theologian Paul Tillich
declared the following:

> People sometimes say, "This is right in theory, but it doesn't work in
> practice." They ought to say, "This is wrong in theory and conse-
> quently it is wrong in practice." There is no true theory which could
> be wrong in practice. This contrast between theory and practice is
> contrived by people who want to escape hard and thorough think-
> ing.... This is true of the history of science, morals and religion."[10]

Certainly, American pragmatists have driven a wedge between theory and
practice in the minds of many people. Within the religious arena, this wedge
represents the distinction between religious belief and spiritual practice.
Gallup research would indicate that the greatest chink in the bulwark of
American religion is the lack of spiritual practices and disciplines actively
exercised by religious adherents. Consider, for instance, the following statistic:
93% of Americans have a copy of the Bible or other Scriptures in their household,
yet only 42% of the nation can name even five of the Ten Commandments.
Spirituality in America may be three thousand miles wide, but it remains only three
inches deep.

PRAYER

Nine out of ten U.S. adults say that they pray. Nearly all who pray think their
prayers are heard (97%) and are answered (95%). Three persons in four pray
daily. An additional 15% of adults claim that they pray at least weekly. Nearly
all who pray believe that their prayers are heard by a supreme being such as
God, Jesus Christ, Jehovah, or the Lord. Some differences in the objects and
subjects of prayer exist according to religious preference. For example,
Protestants are more likely than Catholics to pray for forgiveness (88%), personal salvation (80%), and for their country (80%). Catholics, on the other
hand, are far more likely to pray for relatives who have died (95%). Saying
grace or giving thanks to God before meals appears to be a fairly common
practice in American homes. Protestants are somewhat more likely than
Catholics to say they always or frequently say grace before meals, by a margin
of 56% to 43%.

People pray for myriad reasons. From asking for the family's well-being to
praying for the president and our nation's leaders, Americans offer prayers on
a wide range of topics. Nearly half of those who pray say they started because
of family influences (47%). The family continues to mold people's current

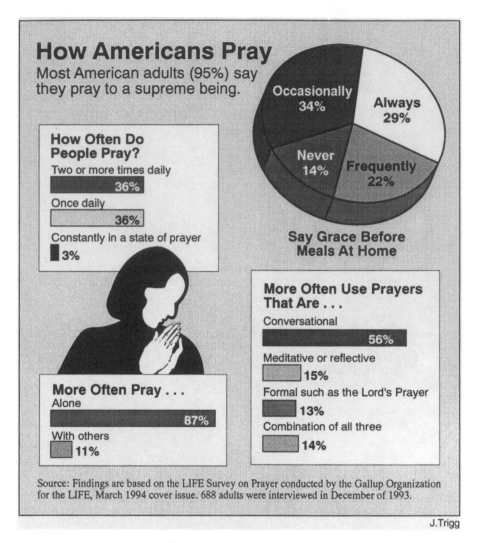

How Americans Pray
Most American adults (95%) say they pray to a supreme being.

How Often Do People Pray?

Two or more times daily
36%

Once daily
36%

Constantly in a state of prayer
3%

More Often Pray . . .
Alone
87%

With others
11%

Occasionally 34%

Always 29%

Never 14%

Frequently 22%

Say Grace Before Meals At Home

More Often Use Prayers That Are . . .

Conversational
56%

Meditative or reflective
15%

Formal such as the Lord's Prayer
13%

Combination of all three
14%

Source: Findings are based on the LIFE Survey on Prayer conducted by the Gallup Organization for the LIFE, March 1994 cover issue. 688 adults were interviewed in December of 1993.

J.Trigg

praying practices. Thirty-four percent of adults in this country report that they pray most often at bedside or in bed; another 23% report praying elsewhere at home. By contrast, only 10% report praying the most when they are in a house of worship. Church influences are reported by one in ten people as the primary cause of prayer, and another 10% say they were led to prayer because of their beliefs. Prayer continues to exercise a pervasive influence over the lives of Americans. Among those who pray, 86% of the people believe that their prayers make them better persons. For most Americans prayer is something that originates in the family, is centered in the home, grows in importance, and generates feelings of peace and hope.

What People Pray For

Nine out of 10 Americans say they pray and 95 percent of those feel their prayers have been answered.

Q. Please tell me if you have ever prayed for each of the following reasons:

Family's well being
98%

World peace
83%

Safe passage on a trip
81%

Loved ones who have died
79%

Your country
76%

The return of Jesus Christ
55%

The president or a political leader
48%

Victory in athletic events
23%

Material things, like winning the lottery, a raise or a new car
18%

For something bad to happen to someone else
5%

Source: Findings are based on the LIFE Survey on Prayer conducted by the Gallup Organization for the LIFE, March 1994 cover issue. 688 adults were interviewed in Daecember of 1993.

J. Trigg

A majority of 55% of those who pray say that, compared to five years ago, prayer is now more important to them. Only 1% say it has become less important, and 43% judge it has remained about the same. Those who worry that young people are becoming less religious will be relieved to discover that young adults lead the nation in supporting the every-increasing importance of prayer.

Most who pray (95%) contend that their petitions have been answered. Among those who say this, nearly all suggest the way they have been answered is in feeling more peaceful (96%) or hopeful (94%). Many declare that they got what they prayed for (62%), and others felt prayer resulted in divine inspiration or a feeling of being led by God (62%). About one in four (23%) reports hearing a voice or seeing a vision as a result of prayer.

In the end, 86% of those who pray believe their prayers make them better persons, and 77% are satisfied with their prayer life.

BIBLE READING

More than nine in ten adults have a copy of Scriptures in their household. More surprisingly, out of the group that owns a Bible, nearly half (47%) report reading it at least on a weekly basis, and some (3%) even read the Bible more than once a day. This represents a dramatic change from years past. In 1986 and 1982 only one in three Americans (33%) read their

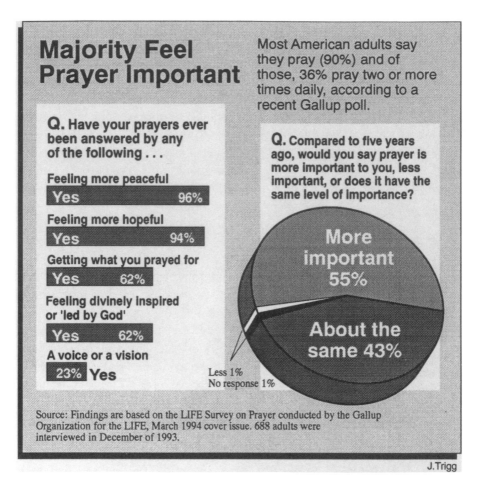

Majority Feel Prayer Important

Most American adults say they pray (90%) and of those, 36% pray two or more times daily, according to a recent Gallup poll.

Q. Have your prayers ever been answered by any of the following . . .

Feeling more peaceful
Yes 96%

Feeling more hopeful
Yes 94%

Getting what you prayed for
Yes 62%

Feeling divinely inspired or 'led by God'
Yes 62%

A voice or a vision
23% Yes

Q. Compared to five years ago, would you say prayer is more important to you, less important, or does it have the same level of importance?

More important 55%

About the same 43%

Less 1%
No response 1%

Source: Findings are based on the LIFE Survey on Prayer conducted by the Gallup Organization for the LIFE, March 1994 cover issue. 688 adults were interviewed in December of 1993.

J.Trigg

Bibles on a weekly basis. In the 1978 survey, 30% reported reading with the same frequency. In addition, the number of people who have never read the Scriptures has dropped in recent years—in 1996, only 16% of adults.

Participation in small groups for Bible study and/or prayer contributes significantly to an individual's chance of reading the Bible frequently. Eighty-eight percent of those Americans who participate in some form of Bible study read their Bibles at least once a week. Among Americans who do not participate in a Bible study group only 27% report reading the Bible at least once during the course of a week. In other words, a chasm of 61 percentage points separates these two groups. Similarly, an overwhelming majority (79%) of Americans involved in some sort of prayer group report reading their Bibles at least once a week.

Distinctions in frequency of Bible reading can also be seen among various faith groups. One of the core issues of the Protestant Reformation of the sixteenth century involved access to Scripture. Martin Luther, John Calvin, and others argued for individuals' reading the Bible in vernacular languages without the interference of priestly interpretation. Protestants today show a remarkably greater inclination to read the Bible on a weekly basis than their Catholic counterparts. Among Protestants in this country, 52% read the Bible

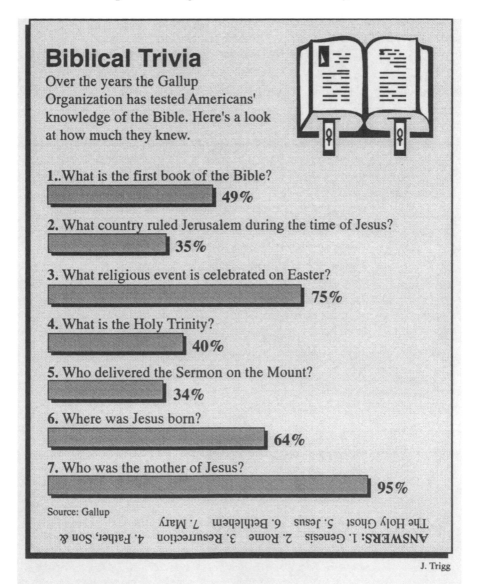

Biblical Trivia

Over the years the Gallup Organization has tested Americans' knowledge of the Bible. Here's a look at how much they knew.

1..What is the first book of the Bible?
49%

2. What country ruled Jerusalem during the time of Jesus?
35%

3. What religious event is celebrated on Easter?
75%

4. What is the Holy Trinity?
40%

5. Who delivered the Sermon on the Mount?
34%

6. Where was Jesus born?
64%

7. Who was the mother of Jesus?
95%

Source: Gallup

ANSWERS: 1. Genesis **2.** Rome **3.** Resurrection **4.** Father, Son & The Holy Ghost **5.** Jesus **6.** Bethlehem **7.** Mary

J. Trigg

at least weekly, and 24% of American Protestants read Scripture on a daily basis. In contrast, 23% of Roman Catholics in this country report reading the Bible weekly, and merely 7% report reading the Bible on a daily basis.

Distinctions also arise between different races and genders. Blacks are almost twice as likely as Whites to read the Bible weekly (64% versus 38%).

America's Most Popular Book

Do you have a Bible or other Scriptures in your household?

	YES	NO
National	93%	7%

Source: Gallup Organization survey conducted for Edelman Communications on behalf of the Church of Jesus Christ of Latter-day Saints, 1997

How often do you read the Bible?
(Asked of Bible owners)

	1996[11]	1986	1982	1978
More than once a day	3%	1%	2%	1%
Daily	18%	10%	13%	11%
Two or three times a week	15%	9%	9%	8%
Weekly	11%	13%	9%	10%
Two or three times a month	7%	6%	5%	4%
Once a month	10%	8%	7%	7%
Less than once a month	19%	26%	25%	28%
Never read the Scriptures	16%	22%	24%	24%
Can't say/ don't know	1%	5%	6%	7%

Source: The Gallup Organization and The Gallup Poll, 1996

While 45% of women read the Bible at least once during the week, only 34% of men claim the same.

The number one reason people read the Bible is that they feel closer to God after reading Holy Scriptures. More than three-quarters of the Bible readers in this country (76%) claim to feel a closer connection with God after reading. By a margin of 81% to 69%, women more readily than men sense an

People Read the Bible to Feel Closer to God

To what extent—a great deal, somewhat, hardly at all, or not at all—has your reading of the Bible affected you in the following ways:

	A GREAT DEAL	SOMEWHAT	HARDLY AT ALL	NOT AT ALL
Has helped me feel closer to God	76%	21%	2%	1%
Has helped me feel at peace	71%	23%	3%	2%
Has helped me find meaning in life	69%	23%	4%	3%
Has led to the Bible's being more meaningful in my life	68%	26%	4%	1%
Has strengthened me to stand up against wrongs in society	66%	26%	5%	2%
Has helped me to be more open and honest about myself	64%	29%	4%	2%
Has given me a new depth of love toward other people	62%	30%	4%	3%

Source: The Gallup Poll, 1998

affinity with God after Scripture reading. Almost all (87%) readers over age 65 experience this close union as a result of their reading the Bible. Four centuries ago, Protestant Reformers sought to provide the laity with access to Holy Scripture. Today, the descendents of these Reformers continue to read the Bible much more than members of the Catholic faith. Protestants are also more apt than Catholics to report feeling closer to God from reading the Bible (79% of Protestants versus 68% of Catholics).

Over seven in ten adults (71%) affirm Bible reading because of the peace it brings to their lives. Young adults disagree, with only 59% of them claiming to feel more peaceful as a result of reading the Bible. Likewise, political independents and ideological moderates do not sense the same measure of peace as a result of reading the Bible that the general population claims. Older Americans (over age 65) sense serenity the most after reading the Bible; 80% of them cite peace as a great benefit of Scripture reading.

The third most popular reason for reading the Bible involves finding meaning in life. Sixty-nine percent of Bible readers believe their time of meditation and study has enabled them to discern purpose and significance for their individual lives. Again, younger adults remain more skeptical than the general population, but still among all subcultures of the population, a strong majority affirm this as a main benefit of Bible reading. This is especially significant for Southerners, conservatives, and Protestants.

Respondents also name other values in reading the Bible. Sixty-eight percent of them believe Scripture reading has led to the Bible becoming more meaningful in their lives. Two-thirds of Bible readers assert that it has also bolstered them to address moral wrongs within society. The majority of Bible readers also find that their reading enables them to be honest and open about themselves, and it gives them greater love toward other people.

Religion Among Blacks

From the "hush harbors" of antebellum South to the gospel and missionary churches that have since spread throughout this country, Black churches have been a substantial force in the ecclesial landscape of the United States. A higher proportion of Blacks take their religion seriously and practice it more ardently in comparison to people of other races.

Blacks in this country are far more likely than Whites to consider religion "very important" in their own lives (82% compared to 58%). Blacks are more likely than Whites to think religion not only is very important but also can answer all or most of today's problems (86% to 62%). Few Blacks or Whites, however, see the impact of religion increasing in this country (27%, each).

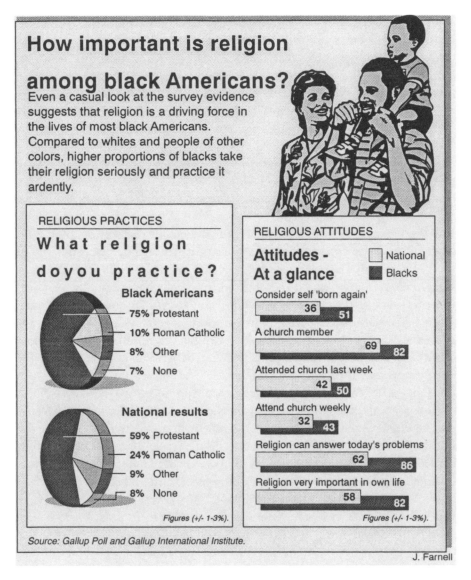

How important is religion among black Americans?

Even a casual look at the survey evidence suggests that religion is a driving force in the lives of most black Americans. Compared to whites and people of other colors, higher proportions of blacks take their religion seriously and practice it ardently.

RELIGIOUS PRACTICES

What religion do you practice?

Black Americans
- 75% Protestant
- 10% Roman Catholic
- 8% Other
- 7% None

National results
- 59% Protestant
- 24% Roman Catholic
- 9% Other
- 8% None

Figures (+/- 1-3%).

RELIGIOUS ATTITUDES

Attitudes - At a glance

☐ National ■ Blacks

Consider self 'born again'
36 / 51

A church member
69 / 82

Attended church last week
42 / 50

Attend church weekly
32 / 43

Religion can answer today's problems
62 / 86

Religion very important in own life
58 / 82

Figures (+/- 1-3%).

Source: Gallup Poll and Gallup International Institute.

J. Farnell

Participation in the affairs of the local church usually is higher among Blacks than Whites. Over eight Blacks in ten (82%) say they are church members, 50% report they attended church at least once during the previous week, and 43% claim church attendance is a weekly practice.

Most Blacks affiliate with and attend worship at a Christian church. Half of American Blacks (51%) assert that they are born-again or evangelical Christians. Three in four (75%) are Protestants, and one in ten (10%) is a

Roman Catholic. Most Protestant Blacks are Southern Baptist (19%) or belong to one of the many other Baptist conventions (22%).

Statistically, just about every Black adult believes in God or a universal spirit. Seven in ten (70%) believe in the devil, and even more think there is a hell (74%). Nearly all Blacks (97%) believe there is a heaven. A very great number of Blacks (85%) say they believe in angels. Three in ten (30%) say they endorse the concept of reincarnation, even though this is contradictory to Christian belief. Some theologians think respondents may be confusing the concept with "born-again" beliefs since reincarnation runs counter to many tenets embraced by Black Americans.

CATHOLIC SPIRITUALITY

In 1998, Pope John Paul II celebrated the twentieth anniversary of his election as the Holy Father of the Roman Catholic Church. Despite the popularity of this pope among Catholics, his teachings and visits have not produced considerable change in Church members' practice of daily spirituality. In fact, there appears to be waning interest in the Church's practices of personal piety—especially among the Church's young people. Only one in three Roman Catholics regularly practice the Church's requirements for personal devotion. While the percentages have altered between the 1970s and the 1990s, a consistent pattern can be traced. For example, one in three Roman Catholics read the Bible over the course of a month. Likewise, 30% of Catholics in the United States say and pray the Rosary during a month. A split among different age groups, however, can be seen on the topic of praying the Rosary. Whereas only 17% of younger Catholics (ages 18 to 29) say that they prayed the Rosary within the last month, nearly half (49%) of Roman Catholics over the age of 50 say that they participated in this practice of their faith. Attendance at confession has slipped to its lowest level in twenty years. In 1993 only 14% reported going to confession within the past thirty days. That figure is even lower (11%) among Catholics who are 18 to 29 years old. Gallup has recognized a trend that has emerged within recent years toward private, personal spirituality, and it is prevalent among all faith groups. As a result, in 1993, Gallup asked Catholics in this country about the practice of praying privately. An astonishing percentage of Catholics (91%) reported praying privately within the last thirty days. This percentage is even higher among middle-age (93%) and older (94%) Catholics.

Despite widespread opposition to many of the Church's teachings and dwindling interest in personal religious practices, vast majorities of both devout and less devout Catholics express satisfaction with the Church's activities. Eighty-five percent say they are at least somewhat satisfied with the Church's fulfillment of their spiritual needs, 83% with the opportunities for them to be involved in the Church, and 74% with the Church's interest in them as individuals.

Personal Piety Wanes Among Catholics

Please tell me whether you, yourself, have done any of the following within the last 30 days.

	1993	1986	1977
Read the Bible	33%	39%	23%
Said (prayed) the Rosary	30%	38%	36%
Attended a Catholic social function	28%	33%	21%
Attended a meeting of a Catholic organization	18%	17%	10%
Gone to confession	14%	23%	18%

Demographic breakdown by age groups for most recent data:

	18–29 years	30–49 years	50 and over
Read the Bible	30%	36%	31%
Said (prayed) the Rosary	17%	24%	49%
Attended a Catholic social function	28%	25%	31%
Attended a meeting of a Catholic organization	21%	17%	18%
Gone to confession	11%	12%	21%

Source: The Gallup Poll and the Gallup Survey for the Catholic Press Association, 1993

FAITH DURING DIFFICULT TIMES

Eight in ten Americans report bouts with depression. Gallup surveyed those who said they experience some form of depression, and the results show a fairly sharp division between those activities that most Americans typically engage in during times of depression and those activities considered to be "very" or "somewhat effective" during those times. For example, nine in ten adults think that talking with friends is an effective way to allay depression, but only 68% of them actually engage in this during difficult times. Even more Americans (94%) think that reading the Bible and spending time in meditation or prayer is needed during tough times. Yet, less than half (48%) report in fact doing one of these as a way to deal with depressive disorders. Ninety-two percent think more time in exercise is helpful in overcoming depression, but only 40% actually exercise when feeling depressed. Almost nine in ten (87%) of adults believe it would be helpful to seek out a pastor or religious leader during times of discouragement, yet less than one-third (27%) of them seek out spiritual guidance. Likewise, seeking help from a doctor or a professional counselor is regarded as effective by seven in ten adults (71%). Here again, however, far fewer people in this country (14%) report frequently or occasionally seeking this assistance in coping with depression.

Ten percent of adults find themselves depressed or discouraged most of the time or quite often, 44% say occasionally, and 26% almost never or never. Women are slightly more likely than men to report depression most of the time or quite often. Young adults (ages 18 to 29) are more inclined to report depression than are older Americans. Money and bills and job-related, family, and health problems are volunteered most often as causes of depression or discouragement, followed by general frustrations, problems with children, the state of the economy, world affairs, and one's social life.

When faced with a personal crisis or problem, eight out of ten Americans pray about the situation. Even more adults (87%) share the issue with their families. Although most Americans say they discuss the problem with their families, eight in ten adults seem to contradict this by claiming that they try to work through the crisis on their own. An overwhelming number of non-Whites (94%) say that they find support during times of crisis through prayer. These coping mechanisms are followed in popularity by talking with close friends and reading the Bible or inspired literature. Formal sources of support such as counselors and support groups are used less frequently. Only 23% of Americans turn to a class or group at their church or synagogue for support during crises.

Religion Lifts Depressed Adults

Please tell me whether you frequently or occasionally do the following when you feel discouraged or depressed and how you rate its effectiveness.

	FREQUENTLY ENGAGE IN THESE ACTIVITIES	SOMEWHAT EFFECTIVE
Spend more time alone, with a hobby, TV, reading, or listening to music	77%	84%
Seek out friends to talk with	68%	90%
Seek out family members to talk with	66%	88%
Eat more/eat less	64%	31%
Spend more time in prayer, meditation, or reading the Bible	48%	94%
Spend more time exercising	40%	92%
Shop more, spend money	31%	47%
Spend more hours at work	29%	77%
Seek out pastor, religious leader	27%	87%
Spend more time sleeping	26%	59%
Seek help from a doctor or professional counselor	14%	71%
Drink more alcohol	10%	37%
Rely more heavily on medication	6%	58%

Source: Gallup Survey for the Christian Broadcasting Network, Inc., 1986

Patterns of response differ widely between genders, with women being less inclined to isolate themselves in critical times and more prone to seeking relational forms of support: friends, religious counselors, or support groups. Women also show greater likelihood to read the Bible and pray about problems. Men, by contrast, fall below the national average in seeking out external forms of support for times of crisis.

People Cope with Crisis Through Family and Prayer

When you are faced with a problem or crisis, to which of the following kinds of support would you likely turn for help?

	NATIONAL	MEN	WOMEN	WHITE	NON-WHITE
Share with family	87%	86%	88%	86%	88%
Prayer	80%	74%	86%	78%	94%
Work it through on your own	80%	85%	75%	80%	79%
Share with close friends	73%	69%	77%	74%	68%
Read Bible or other inspired literature	64%	56%	72%	61%	87%
Religious counselor	40%	35%	46%	38%	55%
Other professional counselor	31%	28%	34%	31%	35%
Support group	26%	22%	29%	24%	34%
Discuss with class or group in church or synagogue	23%	17%	27%	21%	33%

Source: Gallup survey conducted for the Religious Education Association of the United States and Canada, 1985 [12]

Similarly, non-Whites are more likely than Whites to seek counsel from groups, religious counselors, inspirational reading, and especially prayer. Regarding certain forms of support, non-White Americans show a much greater reliance than the national norms. For example, the percentage of non-Whites who read the Bible or inspirational literature during troubling times is twenty-three points higher than the national average. In addition, non-Whites score fifteen points higher than the average American in finding support through the ministry of a religious counselor.

CHARITABLE CONTRIBUTIONS

Americans surpass most other nations in charitable giving, especially in instances of sharing possessions and talents. Most frequently, these charitable impulses are channeled through religious organizations. Nearly three in four Americans (74%) contributed food, clothing, or some other personal property within the past year. Whether contributing to church-based or secular charitable organizations, Americans are much more likely to contribute financially than they are to volunteer their time. On the national level, the percentage of Americans serving as unpaid volunteers for various charities is a dramatic thirty-two points below the percentage of people making donations of food, clothing, or other property (74% compared to 42%). Curiously, even those who are not members of religious organizations make monetary contributions to churches; it is even more surprising to discover that one out of four nonmembers contributed in such a way within the past year.

People in this country offer assistance most often to a relative or friend in need (54% and 53%, respectively). Strangers like homeless and street people are the ones assisted one out of three times (36%) when Americans offer charitable assistance. Americans invest more time and money in aiding disenfranchised members of society—the poor, elderly, infirm, and handicapped—than they do in helping more "mainstream" members of the population who happen to be an occasional victim of crime, abuse, or some kind of disaster. Furthermore, Americans are five times more likely to contribute to the local community (59%) than they are to offer support on the national (11%) or international (12%) level. This is true of church members and nonmembers alike.

Related Gallup research reveals that only one American in three surmises that the rich are now doing an "excellent" or "good" job of giving back to society through charitable contributions and donations. If they were to become rich themselves, almost two Americans in three say they would view charitable contributions as a very important aspect of their stewardship.

Americans Will Give Away Property Before Time

Please tell me if you, yourself, have done the following:

	NATIONAL	CHURCH MEMBERS	NON-MEMBERS

In the past 12 months

	NATIONAL	CHURCH MEMBERS	NON-MEMBERS
Contributed food, clothing, or other property	74%	78%	66%
Made non-church monetary contributions	70%	73%	64%
Made church charity monetary contributions	60%	77%	24%
Served as an unpaid volunteer worker	42%	46%	32%

People directly helped

Needy relative	54%	57%	47%
Needy friend	53%	54%	51%
Needy neighbor	49%	53%	42%
Homeless, street person	36%	37%	33%

People who benefited from direct or indirect help

Poor or homeless	63%	64%	59%
Elderly	62%	68%	50%
Young children	61%	62%	58%
The sick	54%	59%	43%
Victims of crime, abuse or disaster	40%	42%	37%

Areas that benefited

Local community	59%	59%	60%
Nation	11%	10%	12%
World	12%	13%	10%

Source: The Gallup Poll, 1989

RELIGIOUS EDUCATION

Over three-quarters of the adults in this country received some form of religious education as children. The figures jump even higher among the most educated members of our society. Almost all (93%) of Americans with postgraduate education were taught about faith as children. Individuals with a high school education or less fall below the national average on religious training. Twenty-six percent of them did not receive any type of religious education during their childhood or adolescence. This subsection of the populace is the group who received the least amount of religious training in the United States. Nonetheless, even among these people, nearly three-quarters of them (74%) were given some form of religious education during their childhood.

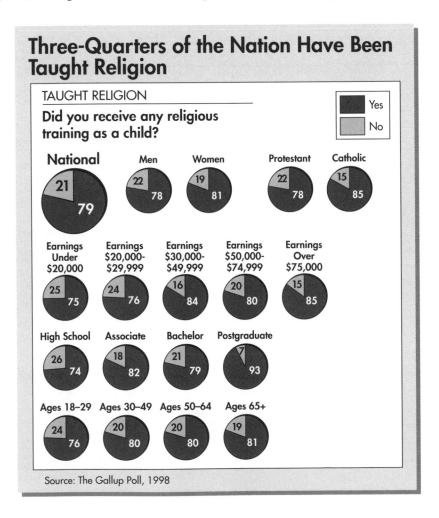

Three-Quarters of the Nation Have Been Taught Religion

TAUGHT RELIGION

Did you receive any religious training as a child?

■ Yes
□ No

National — 21 No, 79 Yes
Men — 22 No, 78 Yes
Women — 19 No, 81 Yes
Protestant — 22 No, 78 Yes
Catholic — 15 No, 85 Yes

Earnings Under $20,000 — 25 No, 75 Yes
Earnings $20,000-$29,999 — 24 No, 76 Yes
Earnings $30,000-$49,999 — 16 No, 84 Yes
Earnings $50,000-$74,999 — 20 No, 80 Yes
Earnings Over $75,000 — 15 No, 85 Yes

High School — 26 No, 74 Yes
Associate — 18 No, 82 Yes
Bachelor — 21 No, 79 Yes
Postgraduate — 7 No, 93 Yes

Ages 18–29 — 24 No, 76 Yes
Ages 30–49 — 20 No, 80 Yes
Ages 50–64 — 20 No, 80 Yes
Ages 65+ — 19 No, 81 Yes

Source: The Gallup Poll, 1998

Ours is a nation of believers, and the findings from this study indicate that inclination toward belief begins at an early age. Nearly all Americans believe in God or a universal spirit. Other Gallup studies reveal a high percentage of Americans who are classified as "churched." Gallup research suggests that this inclination often starts through religious education in childhood. In the past, respondents have mentioned weekly religion classes and parochial schools, as well as parental and familial influence, as sources of religious education. For the vast majority of them (81%), however, the primary locus of religious education was the church through Sunday school programs.

Women as well as Southerners and conservatives are slightly more apt than the general public to have received some form of religious training as children. But most of these percentages are statistically insignificant. One area of distinction worth noting is the disparity between economic classes with regards to childhood religious education. The "haves" in this country are ten percentage points more likely to have received such training than the "have nots." Eighty-five percent of Americans earning over $75,000 experienced religious education as a child. That number drops to 75% among adults earning less than $20,000.

Responses also vary according to age. More of the older members of society were educated on religious matters than the young people of today. By a margin of 81% to 76%, Americans over age 65 were taught about religious matters more often than adults who are currently between the ages of 18 and 29. The Roman Catholic Church's great legacy of religious education also continues to affect Catholics in this country today. Eighty-five percent of U.S. Catholics received religious training during their childhood. Protestants lagged slightly behind with 78% of their members receiving education on matters of faith and practice as children.

Almost nine out of ten Americans (89%) would want a child of theirs to receive some type of religious education. This represents a three-percentage point increase between the 1998 study and a survey conducted a decade earlier. More mature Americans favor religious education for their children than adults who are ages 18 to 29. By a margin of 83% to 93%, these young adults—who are in the prime child-bearing years—express greater reluctance to educate their own children on religious matters than adults over age 65.

People who live in the Midwest (92%) and South (90%) rise above the national average on this question while the population living on the East (86%) and West (85%) Coasts are not as apt to want religious education for their children. Still, an overwhelming majority of all of them favor this.

Similarly, individuals who make less than $30,000 a year are slightly more inclined to favor faith-oriented education and training over wealthier Americans. Republicans (94%) and Democrats (90%) both show strong support for religious education of children while Independents (83%) are less enthusiastic. Eighty-three percent of political Independents responded favorably

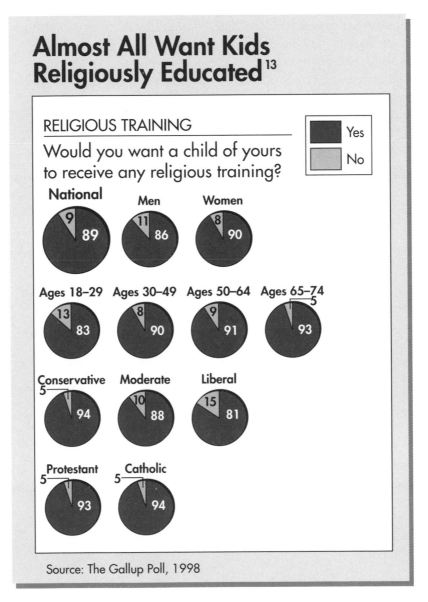

Almost All Want Kids Religiously Educated[13]

RELIGIOUS TRAINING

■ Yes
▨ No

Would you want a child of yours to receive any religious training?

National
9 / 89

Men
11 / 86

Women
8 / 90

Ages 18–29
13 / 83

Ages 30–49
8 / 90

Ages 50–64
9 / 91

Ages 65–74
5 / 93

Conservative
5 / 94

Moderate
10 / 88

Liberal
15 / 81

Protestant
5 / 93

Catholic
5 / 94

Source: The Gallup Poll, 1998

to religious instruction for their children. However, only 81% of ideological liberals—compared with moderates or conservatives—want this type of training for their children.

Both Protestants and Catholics in this country staunchly endorse religious instruction for their children. Almost universal support (96%) has historically been favored among churchgoers in this country, and the 1998 Gallup survey demonstrates continued support for religious education of the next generation.

Religion and Experience

"I myself believe that the evidence for God lies primarily in inner personal experiences."

—William James

American church history has a long legacy of revivalism and spiritual awakenings. Preaching icons like Jonathan Edwards and George Whitefield fortified the American tradition of revival meetings and spiritual awakenings. The first two major religious movements in this country were called the Great Awakenings. Since then, spiritual leaders including D. L. Moody, Billy Sunday, and most recently, Dr. Billy Graham have fanned the flames of religious fervor that originally sparked during the first century of this nation's history. Although many so-called mainline denominations do not conduct regular revival meetings, many "churched" Americans recount such an experience. A number of Americans, 36% in this decade, reported having powerful religious insights or awakenings in these revivals. Figures climb higher among adults who value religion as "extremely" or "very important" in their own lives. Furthermore, even among those people who say that religion is not at all important, 15% reported some type of similar spiritual awakening. Contrary to the critiques offered by skeptics of evangelicalism, Gallup research suggests that changes in faith occur more frequently during times of stability than in crisis. This has led many psychologists of religion to conclude that spiritual transformation—in one form or another—may be innate to the adult life cycle.

Some Americans describe themselves as born again. Nearly four in ten adults (39%) claim to be evangelical believers. Because so many definitions for evangelicalism exist, Gallup listed three main criteria for classification. First, the individual had to regard the Bible as the actual word of God—although belief in its inerrancy is not mandated. Second, the person had to undergo some form of personal conversion. Finally, the respondent had to claim a desire to lead nonbelievers to a point of conversion. When these three parameters were laid out, nearly two out of five Americans responded in the affirmative. Black Americans exceed the national trends for evangelicalism; 58% of them described their spiritual lives as born again. Protestants outdistance

Roman Catholics in number of evangelicals by a margin of 53% to 21%. The largest concentration of born-again believers is found in the South, where 54% of the population is evangelical; the smallest is found in the East, with only 26% of the people claiming an evangelical faith.

The number of people who have experienced the presence of God is double the number of evangelicals in this country. Over four in five adults (82%) have been "very conscious of the presence of God" at some time. Again, percentages are even higher among strong religious adherents; nearly all (97%) who say that religion is extremely important to their lives have sensed God's presence at some time. This type of religious mysticism has surfaced to an even greater extent within recent years. The ecumenical movement of the twentieth century has brought more traditional Western forms of religious piety into an encounter with other strands of spirituality like the Orthodox Church, which has often been praised for its rich legacy of mystical worship. Most Americans experience the divine presence through intellectual, conscious activity. However, 43% of adults report unusual and inexplicable spiritual experiences. These mystical encounters include experiences ranging from out-of-body travel to dreams and visions in which the individual meets God.

Gallup conducted a study in 1985 and then again in 1998 to consider individuals' thought with regards to their relationship to God. In all four areas of inquiry, Americans convey greater interest in matters of faith as they approach the twenty-first century. In 1998, 69% of people in the nation say that they think about the basic meaning and value of their lives a great deal. This figure represents a staggering eleven-point increase in a little over a decade. More Americans are also thinking about living a worthwhile life and developing their faith, as well as about their relationship to God. Perhaps the greatest leap in percentages, however, relates to spiritual growth. In 1984, just over half of the nation (56%) felt the need to experience spiritual growth and development. By 1998 that number leapt an unprecedented twenty-six percentage points. Eighty-two percent of adults now feel the need to grow and mature spiritually. College-educated women, Republicans, conservatives, and Protestants exceed these high national norms with an even greater desire to grow in their faith.

As Americans mature, the likelihood of religion being important intensifies. The national benchmark for importance of religion hovers at 58%. Among Americans over age 50, 70% rank religion as the most important aspect of life. The figure climbs even higher among adults over age 75; three-quarters of them give religion top priority. Moreover, the number of adults this age who think religion is not at all important is half what it was prior to age 50. Comparing our country's senior adults with America's young adults reveals striking contrasts. Whereas 75% of the nation's most senior citizens view religion and faith as important, only 44% of those under age 30 place the same emphasis on religion in their personal lives. In related Gallup research, far fewer young adults call themselves "a religious person." In this survey, respondents are asked to rank themselves on a scale of one to ten. Responding with a score of ten means the individual regards "a religious person" as a "perfect description" of their lives; only 18% of the country place themselves in this category. The percentage giving themselves a ten increases steadily with age, which suggests a positive correlation between spiritual development and maturity.

In sum, the spiritual thermostat of this country has always been turned a bit warmer than other nations. From the fiery preaching of Jonathan Edwards to the current generation's passionate interest in individual spirituality, the United States is a nation that has been characterized by religious zeal and fervor. The proliferation of faith-centered small groups and increasing interest in spiritual growth will lead to even further spiritual enthusiasm in the coming century.

Born-Again Experiences

Nearly four in ten Americans (39%) describe themselves as born-again or evangelical Christians. The evangelical movement cuts across denominational boundaries and shares a prominent place in the nation's religious mainstream. By Gallup's definition, a born-again or evangelical Christian believes that the Bible is the actual word of God, has experienced personal conversion, and seeks to lead non-Christians to conversion. Most likely to describe themselves this way are women, persons 65 and older, and people living in rural areas. In addition, Blacks are much more likely than Whites to classify themselves as evangelical. Twenty percentage points separate the Black population who are evangelical and White evangelicals. Furthermore, by a two-to-one margin, more Southerners profess to be born again than folks living in the East (54% versus 26%).

The number of Americans who claim to be evangelical has remained constant between 1976 and 1996. For the most part, beliefs among various subcultures of the American population remained unchanged during that period. One exception can be seen among the nation's Catholics. Whereas in 1988 only 12% of Catholics described themselves as born again or evangelical, eight years later 21% of Catholics claimed to be evangelical. Protestant churches in the United States, however, continued to claim the majority of this country's evangelicals. In 1988, 49% of Protestants said they were born again, and in 1996 53% of Protestants made the same claim.

Born-Again Experience Pervades

EXPERIENCES OF CHRISTIANS

Would you describe yourself as a "born-again" or evangelical Christian, or not? That is, do you believe the Bible is the actual Word of God, have you experienced a personal conversion, and do you seek to lead non-Christians to conversion?

	Yes, I am "born again"
National	39%
Men	37%
Women	41%
White	38%
Black	58%
East	26%
Midwest	37%
South	54%
West	36%
Protestant	53%
Catholic	21%
1996	39%
1995	42%
1992	36%
1988	33%
1983	38%
1981	35%
1976	38%

Source: The Gallup Poll, 1996

Revivalism and religious experience in this country date back to the First and Second Great Awakenings of the eighteenth and nineteenth centuries. Contemporary evangelicalism has been gaining momentum among Americans since the early 1970s. With this movement more Americans have claimed religious experiences or moments of intense religious insight. However, experiences of God occur widely outside evangelical communities. Even among those adults who say that religion is "not too important" or "not at all important," 15% have experienced some type of religious awakening. The

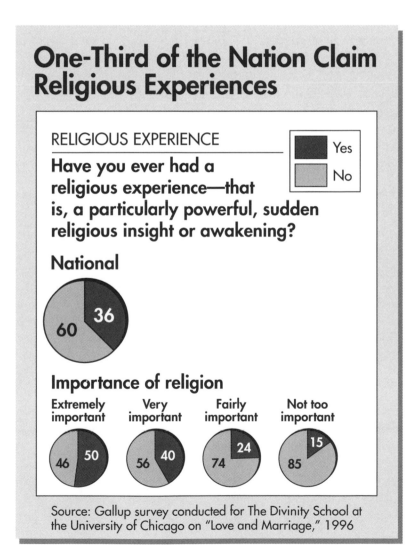

One-Third of the Nation Claim Religious Experiences

RELIGIOUS EXPERIENCE

Have you ever had a religious experience—that is, a particularly powerful, sudden religious insight or awakening?

■ Yes
▨ No

National

36
60

Importance of religion

Extremely important	Very important	Fairly important	Not too important
50 / 46	40 / 56	24 / 74	15 / 85

Source: Gallup survey conducted for The Divinity School at the University of Chicago on "Love and Marriage," 1996

number jumps to nearly one in four adults (24%) among those who say that religion is "fairly important" in their lives. The figures become even higher among those Americans who say that religion is "very" or "extremely important." One out of two adults in this country who believe religion is extremely important claim they have had a religious experience.

The national average on spiritual awakenings in 1996 was slightly higher than a decade earlier. In the 1980s, 33% of Americans said that they had encountered a "powerful religious insight or awakening" at some point in their lives. Since then, the number has increased three percentage points to 36%. In a related question in the same study, 57% of Americans reported having an important religious experience that reinforced their faith. Among those Americans who regard religion as "extremely important," the figure jumps to 81%. The number of adults who do not claim such an experience corresponds with the importance of religion in individuals' lives. For example, among those who consider religion as "fairly important," 38% of Americans have had a religious experience that reinforced their faith. For those who say religion is "not too important" or "not at all important," only 11% underwent such an experience.

SELF-RELIANCE

American legends of self-made individuals such as Horatio Alger exemplify many ideals of this country—independence, hard work, self-confidence, and commitment. Previous generations seemed to temper the glorification of self-reliance with an acknowledgment of divine assistance and providence. As we near the end of the twentieth century, however, Americans' opinions have shifted. Adults in this country place more trust in themselves than on outside powers—such as God—to solve the problems of life. Fifty-four percent of U.S. adults claim to rely more upon themselves to answer life's challenges than on any other means of support. Just over one-third of the country (35%) draws upon divine assistance when facing major problems in life. Today, no subculture of the U.S. population places the *majority* of its trust in an outside power such as God, but among certain groups, a *plurality* rely the most upon providential aid.

As Americans grow older, reliance upon self wanes, and more depend upon God or other outside powers for support. For example, 65% of the nation's young adults (ages 18 to 29) place the preponderance of trust in the individual self with less than one-third relying mostly upon God (28%). But by the time Americans reach retirement age (over age 65), the plurality of people trust God to solve their major life problems (45%).

Self-Reliant People Predominate

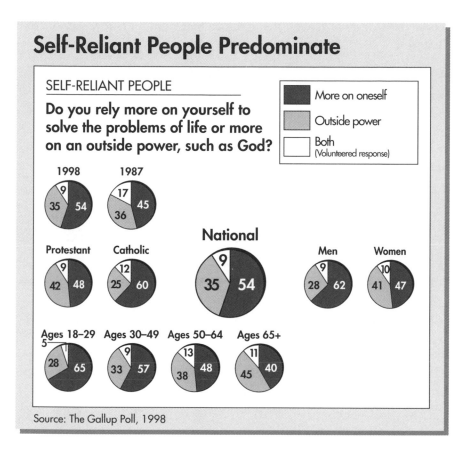

SELF-RELIANT PEOPLE

Do you rely more on yourself to solve the problems of life or more on an outside power, such as God?

More on oneself

Outside power

Both
(Volunteered response)

1998   1987

9 35 54   17 36 45

Protestant   Catholic   **National**   Men   Women

9 42 48   12 25 60   9 35 54   9 28 62   10 41 47

Ages 18–29   Ages 30–49   Ages 50–64   Ages 65+

5 28 65   9 33 57   13 38 48   11 45 40

Source: The Gallup Poll, 1998

Americans with postgraduate education and/or college degrees are more self-reliant than the general population. Two in three adults (67%) with postgraduate schooling and 61% of people with college degrees depend mostly upon themselves to solve these major life challenges. However, education alone does not determine an individual's opinion on the matter. For example, men without college degrees still remain more likely to be self-reliant than women without university education, by a margin of 60% (non-collegiate-trained men) to 52% (college-educated women).

Nearly one-half of the conservatives in the United States (48%) rely on God to tackle the major problems of life. Yet a strong contingency (42%) continue to depend mostly upon themselves. Moderates and, to an even greater degree, liberals primarily count on themselves to solve these major dilemmas. Roman Catholics follow the pattern of liberals in this country on this issue. Only one-quarter of U.S. Catholics say that they rely on an outside power such as God; 60% of them rely on themselves when faced with adversity or troubling times.

CONSCIOUS OF GOD

Eight out of ten Americans (82%) agree that they are "sometimes very conscious of the presence of God," with far fewer, 17%, who say they are not. Americans in the 1990s demonstrate a greater inclination toward mystical beliefs and practices than they did even ten years earlier. While religious mysticism can be traced back to great figures in church history such as Teresa of

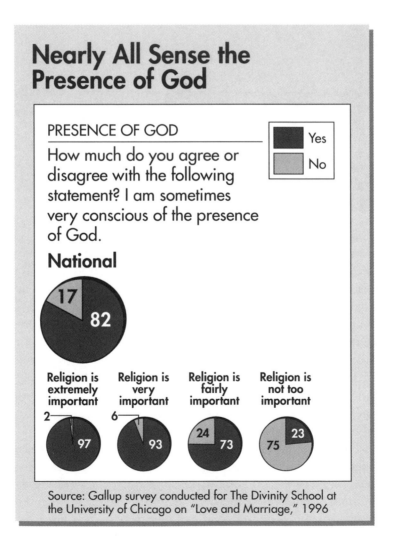

Nearly All Sense the Presence of God

PRESENCE OF GOD

How much do you agree or disagree with the following statement? I am sometimes very conscious of the presence of God.

■ Yes
□ No

National

17
82

Religion is extremely important	Religion is very important	Religion is fairly important	Religion is not too important
2 / 97	6 / 93	24 / 73	75 / 23

Source: Gallup survey conducted for The Divinity School at the University of Chicago on "Love and Marriage," 1996

Avila, more people today are expressing a conscious mystical awareness of the divine than ever before. Certain segments of the population demonstrate an even higher propensity to express this consciousness—especially women, persons over 50, and Blacks. By religious affiliation, evangelical Protestants are most inclined to report awareness of a divine presence. Spirituality among Americans clearly extends beyond the confines of organized religion. Importance of religion corresponds with, but does not mandate, an individual's experience. One out of five adults, for example, who say that religion is either "not too important" or "not at all important" still report that they are sometimes aware of God's presence.

The figure skyrockets among the next category of Americans; 73% of those who rank religion as "fairly important" indicate a consciousness of God's presence. Essentially, all Americans who believe that religion is extremely important or very important for their individual lives experience an awareness of the divine (97% and 93%, respectively). In a related Gallup survey, a remarkable 43% of Americans reported unusual and inexplicable spiritual or religious experiences of profound and positive impact, ranging from out-of-body travel to visionary encounters.[14] Descriptions of these spiritual experiences include a sense of divine presence and guidance, peace, extrasensory perception, answered prayer, and renewed strength.

Americans tend to take their religion fairly seriously to start with, but the tendency becomes even stronger as they grow older. Overall, a majority of adults in this country (58%) see religion as being "extremely" or "very important" to them, and an additional 29% consider it "somewhat important." Among those who are under age 30, over four in ten (44%) say it is at least very important. By the time they reach the 30-to-49-years-of-age bracket, over half (54%) claim to take religion very seriously. This finding contradicts what many forecasters suggested about the religious indifference of the Baby Boomers. By age 50 about seven persons in ten judge religion to be extremely or very important. At the other extreme, the number in this age group who rate it unimportant is cut in half. By age 75, interest in religion peaks with three persons in four (75%) saying it is extremely or very important to them.

Women of all ages are more likely than men to consider religion very important, by a margin of 65% to 50%. Blacks are more inclined than Whites to focus on religion (82% compared to 55%). The South leads all regions of the country in the proportion of people who take their religion very seriously (68%); the West lags farthest behind (48%). Religious feelings run stronger in small towns and rural areas (65%) than in large cities and their suburbs (55%). Protestants more often than Catholics esteem religion as very important (65% to

Religion's Importance Intensifies as People Grow Older

How important is religion in your own life—extremely important, very important, moderately important, only somewhat important, or not at all important?

	EXTREMELY	VERY
National	30%	28%
Male	24	26
Female	35	30
Ages18-29	22	22
Ages 30-49	28	26
Ages 50-64	35	31
White	29	26
Black	47	35
Protestant	34	31
Roman Catholic	22	29
East	26	25
Midwest	31	33
South	36	32
West	26	22

Source: The Gallup Organization, 1994   — = under 1%

51%). Very strong feelings also are noted among those who describe themselves as members of the Religious Right (88%) or as born-again Christians (79%).

A related study in 1994 by the George H. Gallup International Institute approached the question of importance somewhat differently and elicited responses from one-third of the adult population that they felt religion is "extremely important" in their lives. An additional one-third said it is very important, while 25% reported religion is only fairly important, and 9% said it is not at all important to them. Most likely to consider religion extremely important in their lives are Blacks (53%) and people who are age 65 and older (40%).

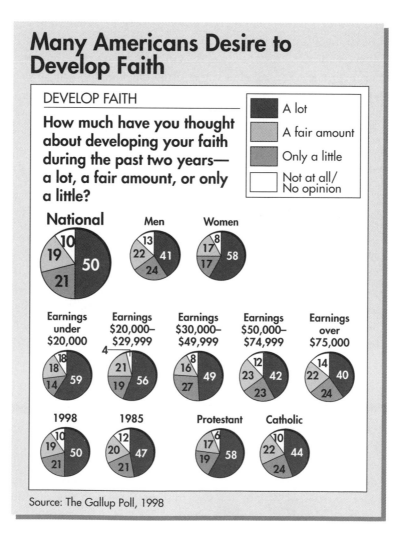

Many Americans Desire to Develop Faith

DEVELOP FAITH

How much have you thought about developing your faith during the past two years— a lot, a fair amount, or only a little?

- ■ A lot
- ▨ A fair amount
- ▧ Only a little
- □ Not at all/ No opinion

National
10, 19, 21, 50

Men
13, 22, 24, 41

Women
8, 17, 17, 58

Earnings under $20,000
18, 18, 14, 59

Earnings $20,000– $29,999
4, 21, 19, 56

Earnings $30,000– $49,999
8, 16, 27, 49

Earnings $50,000– $74,999
12, 23, 23, 42

Earnings over $75,000
14, 22, 24, 40

1998
10, 19, 21, 50

1985
12, 20, 21, 47

Protestant
6, 17, 19, 58

Catholic
10, 22, 24, 44

Source: The Gallup Poll, 1998

One in two Americans thinks often about developing his or her individual faith. The statistics at the end of the twentieth century reflect slightly higher interest in personal faith than existed during the previous decade. A strong majority of people in this nation (71%) reflect on developing individual faith with some degree of frequency. Striking discrepancies, however, surface between men and women. Forty-one percent of men often think about developing their personal faith. By contrast, 58% of women—a remarkable seventeen percentage points higher than men—ponder personal faith with the same degree of frequency. And whereas 13% of men say that they don't think about developing their faith at all, only 8% of women make the same claim.

Age also affects individual interest in developing personal faith. Forty-six percent of young adults in this country (ages 18 to 29) often consider how to deepen their faith many times during the course of two years. But even more Americans over age 65 think about it as often; 58% of this country's senior adults frequently think about maturing in the faith.

Four in ten college-educated men in this country consider how to develop their personal faith on a frequent basis, and 13% of them say that they do not think about such matters at all. At the opposite end of the spectrum, women without college education think about growing in personal faith much more. Six in ten of them claim to have reflected on deepening personal faith "a lot" over the past two years. Personal income also affects differences of opinion. People earning over $75,000 a year think about developing their faith much less often than people earning less than $20,000 a year. Again, the differences are spread out over twenty percentage points. Forty percent of the nation's wealthiest individuals contemplate developing personal faith often. But 59% of people earning less than $20,000 each year reflect on the matter with the same regularity. Finally, Protestants think about maturing in personal faith much more often than Roman Catholics. Nearly three in five Protestants (58%) say they think about it "a lot" whereas only 44% of Catholics claim to do the same.

Relationship to God

Nearly three in five U.S. adults (58%) consider their relationship to God on a regular basis. Another 21% think about this topic "a fair amount." With nearly four-fifths of the population giving ample reflection on their relationship to God, it is not surprising that the United States is regarded as the most religious nation of the industrialized world. Despite recent clamor about the nation's indifference to matters of faith, the vast majority of Americans demonstrate interest in the divine-human relationship.

Most Adults Interested in Relationship to God

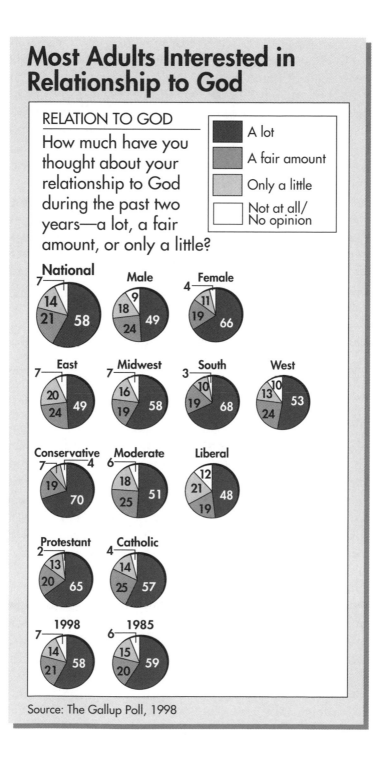

RELATION TO GOD

How much have you thought about your relationship to God during the past two years—a lot, a fair amount, or only a little?

- A lot
- A fair amount
- Only a little
- Not at all/No opinion

National
7, 14, 21, 58

Male
9, 18, 24, 49

Female
4, 11, 19, 66

East
7, 20, 24, 49

Midwest
7, 16, 19, 58

South
3, 10, 19, 68

West
10, 13, 24, 53

Conservative
7, 4, 19, 70

Moderate
6, 18, 25, 51

Liberal
12, 21, 19, 48

Protestant
2, 13, 20, 65

Catholic
4, 14, 25, 57

1998
7, 14, 21, 58

1985
6, 15, 20, 59

Source: The Gallup Poll, 1998

American women show tremendous interest in their relationship with God. Two out of three women in this country say that they think about this relationship "a lot." Men, on the other hand, do not exemplify the same religious fervor. Just under half of the men in this country (49%) contemplate their relationship with God frequently. College-educated men think about it slightly less. Levels of income also affect one's likelihood to think about faith matters on a regular basis. Wealthier Americans do not spend nearly the amount of time thinking about these types of things as do Americans with average or below-average incomes.

Fourteen percentage points divide this nation's young and senior adults. While 56% of 18- to 29-year-olds suggest that they think about God "a lot," 70% of the country's senior adults (over age 65) claim to do the same. Disparity also surfaces between differing ideological groups. Seven in ten conservatives fall into the top category of thinking about one's relationship with God. Less than half of liberals (48%), by contrast, do the same. Likewise, liberals are three times as likely as conservatives to say that they do not think about their relationship with God at all (12% versus 4%).

Protestants are slightly more inclined than Catholics to think about their relationship to God. Sixty-five percent of this country's Protestants ponder the divine-human relationship "a lot." Fifty-seven percent of U.S. Catholics fall into the same category of frequency.

SPIRITUAL GROWTH

Nearly eight in ten Americans (82%) believe that they need to experience spiritual growth. People of all major faith groups in the United States today pursue ways to deepen their religious convictions and strengthen their spiritual practices. In 1998 the producers of PBS's "Religion and Ethics Newsweekly" released their choices for the top twenty-five religious figures of the twentieth century. They include (listed alphabetically) Swiss pastor and theologian Karl Barth; German pastor and theologian Dietrich Bonhoeffer; Jewish theologian Martin Buber; the fourteenth Dalai Lama; Dorothy Day, pacifist and founder of the Catholic Worker Movement and newspaper; Christian Science founder Mary Baker Eddy; Mohandas Gandhi; Billy Graham; Gustavo Gutierrez, Peruvian priest and founder of liberation theology; Carl F. H. Henry, evangelical theologian and founder of *Christianity Today*; rabbi and civil rights activist Abraham Joshua Heschel; Popes John XXIII and John Paul II; Martin Luther King, Jr.; Ayatollah Khomeni; writers C. S. Lewis and Thomas Merton; Elijah Muhammed, founder of the Nation of Islam; Protestant theologian Reinhold Niebuhr; Norman Vincent Peale; Walter Rauschenbusch, founder of the social gospel; Albert Schweitzer; Hasidic Jewish leader Menachem Mendel Schneerson; Mother Theresa; and writer Elie Wiesel, a Holocaust survivor.

As we approach the end of a century influenced by many of these great religious leaders, more Americans express interest in growing spiritually than ever before. Almost every subgroup of the populace expresses this desire intently. Southerners, highly educated individuals, and Protestants rise above the national average in support of further spiritual growth and development. Nearly nine in ten Republicans (89%) and college-educated women (88%) sense the urgency to grow spiritually. In fact, the people who express the least

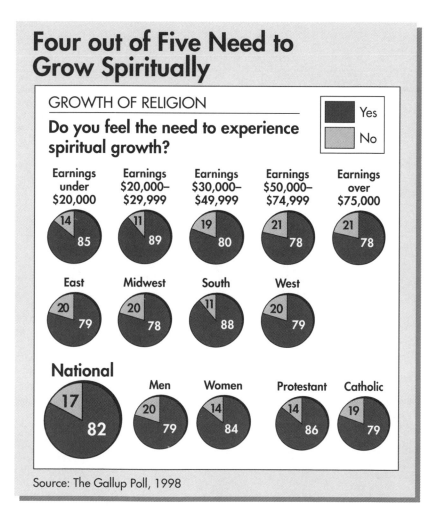

Four out of Five Need to Grow Spiritually

GROWTH OF RELIGION

Do you feel the need to experience spiritual growth?

■ Yes
▢ No

Earnings under $20,000	Earnings $20,000–$29,999	Earnings $30,000–$49,999	Earnings $50,000–$74,999	Earnings over $75,000
14 / 85	11 / 89	19 / 80	21 / 78	21 / 78

East	Midwest	South	West
20 / 79	20 / 78	11 / 88	20 / 79

National 17 / 82

Men	Women	Protestant	Catholic
20 / 79	14 / 84	14 / 86	19 / 79

Source: The Gallup Poll, 1998

amount of interest in growing in matters of faith—political independents and Americans earning more than $50,000 a year—still demonstrate staunch support for spiritual development. Seventy-six percent and 78% of those groups, respectively, perceive the need for further spiritual growth. Although religious leaders continue to disagree on the best way in which this spiritual growth can germinate and flourish, it is clear that an overwhelming number of Americans are eager for spiritual planting and growth.

Religion and Attitudes toward the Church

A woman went into a Häagen-Dazs store in Kansas City for an ice-cream cone. She got her ice cream, turned, and found herself face to face with actor Paul Newman. He smiled and said hello. She stammered something and left the shop, heart pounding. Then she realized that she did not have her ice cream. She started back into the store to get it and met Newman at the door. "Are you looking for your ice cream?" he asked. She nodded. "You put it in your purse with your change," he told her.[15]

We live in a time that idolizes our celebrities. Some American churches feel that they struggle to compete with the glitzy glamour that bombards popular culture. Many religious leaders and pastors think that they must abandon their tradition's style of worship and ecclesiology in order to woo the general public. "Seeker-sensitive" and "user-friendly" churches loom largely over the nation's religious landscape. Many faith communities now follow the successful models for ministry, worship, and church growth that megachurches like Willow Creek Community Church outside of Chicago pioneered two decades ago. Obviously, churches must make adjustments and improvements lest they lose step with the world in which their parishioners live and work.

The Roman Catholic Church introduced sweeping changes during the middle of this century with the Second Vatican Council conducted in the early 1960s. Many American Catholics, however, want the Church to further modify its policies and practices. Take, for instance, opinions on birth control. A monumental majority of Catholics in this country (84%) endorse Church members being able to practice artificial means of birth control. Eighty-two percent of Church members believe one can practice artificial birth control and still be a good Catholic. On another topic, 78% support divorced Catholics being permitted to remarry in the Catholic Church. Roughly two-thirds of American Catholics support women's ordination to the priesthood. This figure has more than doubled over the past twenty years, and in just eight years, the number climbed eleven percentage points to its current approval rating of 63%. Furthermore, three in four Catholics favor the Church's sanctioning priests to marry. This statistic also has also grown since earlier surveys. In 1971, the figure rested at 49%, and it has grown ever since.

Despite these disagreements, most Catholics in the United States continue to support the Church's position on homosexuality. Only one out of three Catholics (35%) believe that those who practice homosexual acts can still be good Catholics. There is further disapproval of homosexuals in ministry among all faith groups. Within the last three years, however, approval for homosexual members of the clergy has eked past the halfway mark. In 1996, 53% of the nation approved of homosexuals being hired for clergy posts. The number of Americans who hold an absolute resistance to homosexuals in the ministry has declined in recent years (40% in 1996 versus 54% in 1977). Americans express much greater acceptance of hiring homosexuals as sales associates, members of the armed forces, or even the president's cabinet. The United Church of Christ is the only "mainline" denomination that has yet approved the ordination of practicing homosexuals for ministry positions, although in their church polity, the final decision is made by the local congregation.

Eighty percent of the country believes that churches today understand the real spiritual nature of religion. Two out of three Americans (67%) affirm the church's success in helping people find meaning for their lives. Sixty-four percent of the population praises the church for welcoming strangers and outsiders. In addition to these praises, the people of this country exhort the church to diminish its emphasis on organizational matters—to focus more on people and less on internal politics. Americans further admonish U.S. churches to pursue matters of social justice.

One of the most prominent features of the ecclesial landscape within recent years involves the emergence of faith-based small groups. A staggering number of Americans—100 million and growing—participate in these on a regular basis. Nearly seven in ten (69%) small groups in this country include prayer. Sixty-three percent of them discuss religious topics. Over half (56%) of the small group meetings in this country involve the study and discussion of Scripture. There could be nearly one million Bible study groups shortly after the year 2000. A 1991 study conducted by the George H. Gallup International Institute in conjunction with Princeton University sociologist Robert Wuthnow estimated that there were 800,000 adult Sunday school classes in this country at that time. Nearly half (46%) of small group members stated their purpose in joining centered around a desire to develop a more disciplined spiritual life. Forty-three percent of small group members heard about the gathering through their church or synagogue. Fifty-seven percent characterize small group meetings as a regular activity of their place of worship. Indeed, small groups influence the spiritual development of Americans today.

Participation in local houses of worship has remained steady over the last several decades. Forty-four percent of the country falls into the "unchurched" category. By Gallup Poll definition, this means that the individual does not claim membership in a local congregation and/or has not attended religious services within the past six months with the exception of special occasions such as weddings, funerals, and holiday services. Men are more inclined than women to be unchurched. The number of "churched" individuals peaks among Black Americans, adults over the age of 65, Southerners, and conservatives. Despite these findings, the United States remains one of the most "churched" nations of the industrialized world. And when compared with the rest of the world, Americans rate their churches much higher. An international Gallup study conducted a few years ago revealed that 73% of U.S. adults felt their churches were meeting spiritual needs, the highest ranking of the nations surveyed.

Catholicism in America

A slight majority (54%) of U.S. Catholics describe their faith as "strong." Only about one Catholic in four would use the self-descriptor "very strong Catholic." Feelings of Catholic identity intensify as believers grow older. People over 50 form the largest category of Catholics who describe their faith as very strong. Catholics who are ages 18 to 29 express the most reluctance to describe their faith in similar terms (only 12%). Although 43% of Catholics say that they and their parents attach equal importance to their faith, 36% deem faith less important to them than it is to their parents. Moreover, only 13% think it more important to them than to their parents. Younger Catholics are twice as likely as those over 50 to respond that their Catholic faith is less important to them than it is for the previous generation.

Pope John Paul II is personally popular with U.S. Catholics of all ages. His 1993 visit to Denver for the World Youth Day festival attested to his popularity among today's younger Catholics. About three Catholics in four (73%) approve of the way he leads and guides their Church. On questions of morality, however, most U.S. Catholics (79%) say they are far more likely to follow the dictates of their own conscience than the teachings of the Pope (16%). An additional 5% volunteered that they would attempt to reconcile the two. Among Catholics under age 50, 85% would follow their own consciences and just 10% would adhere to papal dogma.

Gallup surveys underscore unmistakable differences of opinion between U.S. Catholics and Rome. For example, most American Catholics (78%) support permitting divorced Catholics to remarry in the Catholic Church. Six in ten believe that those who are divorced and remarry without an annulment can still be good Catholics. U.S. Catholics argue even more against the teachings of the Church on the issue of birth control. Currently, 84% believe Catholics should be allowed to practice artificial means of birth control. Even among those who consider themselves as very strong Catholics and who say that they agree with the Church on all matters of morality, a majority argue for loosening the current strictures. Eighty-nine percent believe people can practice artificial birth control and still be good Catholics. Additionally, a majority of Catholics (58%) believe their Church should relax its standards forbidding all abortions. Half (51%) say a woman can have an abortion and still be a good Catholic. There is, however, one matter of greater agreement between Rome and this country's Catholics. Regarding homosexuality, only one Catholic in three (35%) believes those who practice homosexual acts can still be good Catholics.

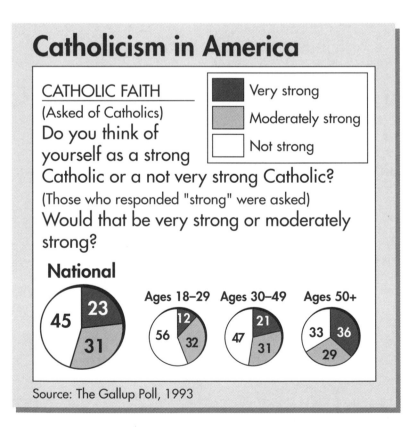

Catholicism in America

CATHOLIC FAITH
(Asked of Catholics)
Do you think of yourself as a strong Catholic or a not very strong Catholic?
(Those who responded "strong" were asked)
Would that be very strong or moderately strong?

■ Very strong
▨ Moderately strong
□ Not strong

National

45 23 31

Ages 18–29
56 12 32

Ages 30–49
47 21 31

Ages 50+
33 36 29

Source: The Gallup Poll, 1993

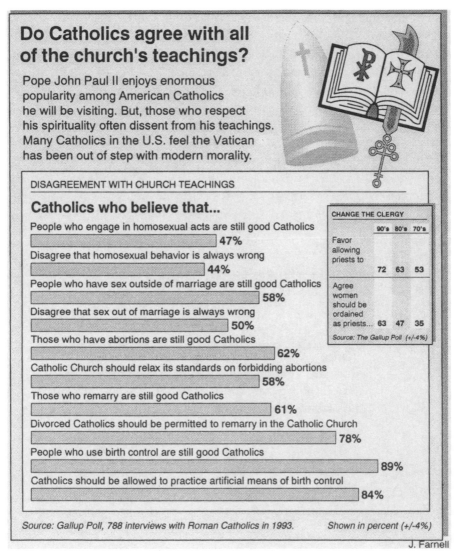

Do Catholics agree with all of the church's teachings?

Pope John Paul II enjoys enormous popularity among American Catholics he will be visiting. But, those who respect his spirituality often dissent from his teachings. Many Catholics in the U.S. feel the Vatican has been out of step with modern morality.

DISAGREEMENT WITH CHURCH TEACHINGS

Catholics who believe that...

People who engage in homosexual acts are still good Catholics **47%**

Disagree that homosexual behavior is always wrong **44%**

People who have sex outside of marriage are still good Catholics **58%**

Disagree that sex out of marriage is always wrong **50%**

Those who have abortions are still good Catholics **62%**

Catholic Church should relax its standards on forbidding abortions **58%**

Those who remarry are still good Catholics **61%**

Divorced Catholics should be permitted to remarry in the Catholic Church **78%**

People who use birth control are still good Catholics **89%**

Catholics should be allowed to practice artificial means of birth control **84%**

CHANGE THE CLERGY

	90's	80's	70's
Favor allowing priests to	72	63	53
Agree women should be ordained as priests...	63	47	35

Source: The Gallup Poll (+/-4%)

Source: Gallup Poll, 788 interviews with Roman Catholics in 1993.   Shown in percent (+/-4%)

J. Farnell

Support among Catholics for the ordination of women as priests has steadily increased since 1974. Gallup's most recent study, conducted in 1993, showed that nearly two in three American Catholics favor females being ordained to the priesthood. Of these Catholics, 33% strongly agree that this should be done and 30% express modest agreement. Among younger Catholics—those under age 30—three in four endorse the ordination of women (76%), compared to 67% of those who are 30 to 49 years of age, and just 48% of those who are 50 and older.

Nearly half (48%) of the Catholics interviewed believe their Church has not gone far enough in adopting modern ideas on women's roles in society. Of the remaining people, 40% consider the Church's position to be about right in this respect, and just 6% feel it has gone too far. Younger Catholics are more likely than those 50 and older to believe their Church must modernize its attitudes. Among women, themselves, 47% feel the Church has to take further steps to recognize their modern role in society, and 63% endorse the ordination of women as priests.

In a related survey, Gallup research showed that three in four U.S. Catholics of all ages now favor allowing Catholic priests to marry and continue to function as priests. Support for this reform in the Catholic Church has grown steadily since 1971 when the figure rested at 49%. In 1973, the number

Two in Three Catholics Support Women's Ordination

WOMEN'S ORDINATION

Please tell me how much you agree or disagree with this statement: It would be a good thing if women were allowed to be ordained as priests.

Note: Question asked of Roman Catholics

	Yes, it would be a good thing
1993	63%
1985 [16]	52%
1982	46%
1979	40%
1977	36%
1974 [17]	29%

Source: The Gallup Poll, National Opinion Research Center, and NY Times/CBS News Poll, 1993 and 1985

climbed to 57%. By 1983, 62% of Americans who practiced the Catholic faith favored allowing priests to marry. In 1993 the number had reached 75%.

GAYS IN MINISTRY

The idea of homosexuals as clergy is gaining more and more acceptance. Over half (53%) of American adults support homosexuals being hired for clergy positions. This figure has changed significantly over the past twenty years. In 1977 only 36% of people in this country affirmed homosexual members of the clergy. Likewise, the number of Americans who hold an absolute feeling against homosexuals in the ministry has decreased (40% in 1996 compared to 54% in 1977).

Despite the recent increase in approval for homosexuals in local parish work, however, Americans remain reluctant to fully endorse the idea. Although more Americans believe that homosexuals should have equal rights in the job market, many continue to draw the line when it comes to hiring homosexuals for the church. Overall, 84% of American adults think that homosexual men and women should enjoy job opportunities equal to the general population. Yet only 53%

Americans Draw the Line on Gays in Ministry

HOMOSEXUAL CLERGY

Do you think homosexuals should or should not be hired as clergy?

	Yes	No
1996	53%	40%
1992	43%	50%
1987	42%	51%
1985	41%	53%
1977	36%	54%

Source: The Gallup Poll, 1996

Do you think homosexuals should or should not be hired for each of the following occupations?

	Should	Should not
Salesperson	90%	7%
Member of the armed forces	65%	29%
Doctor	69%	25%
Elementary school teacher	55%	40%
High school teacher	60%	34%
Member of the President's cabinet	71%	24%

Source: The Gallup Poll, 1996

of the people suggest that they should be hired as ministers. Americans express greater acceptance of hiring homosexuals as salespersons, members of the armed forces, doctors, and even members of the President's cabinet. The current close division of opinion between those who think homosexuals should enjoy equal opportunity when the clergy are hired (53%) and those who do not (40%) mirrors the controversies that have taken place at several denominational meetings within recent years. At annual meetings during the 1990s, many faith groups, including Anglicans, Methodists, Presbyterians, and Southern Baptists, have debated the issue of homosexuals in ministry, particularly ordained ministry. None of those groups as denominational bodies has yet affirmed the ordination of homosexuals. The United Church of Christ General Synod has encouraged individual congregations to be "open and affirming" of individuals for membership and for ministry without regard to sexual preference, but the final decision for ordination among UCC churches lies with individual congregations.

Religious beliefs play an important role in this issue. Those Americans who consider religion very important in their individual lives are less likely than the general population to endorse homosexuals in the clergy (44% compared with 53%). By contrast, 71% of adults who regard religion as "not very important" in their individual lives endorse homosexuals having equal access to ministry posts. Differences of opinion become most striking among individuals with different understandings of the cause of homosexuality. For example, among adults who believe that homosexuality is a predisposition at birth, 73% affirm homosexuals in the ordained clergy. That figure splits in half (34%) for those adults who believe homosexuality is caused by individual choice and upbringing.

ORGANIZED RELIGION

According to Gallup research, the American people offer several critiques and admonitions for the American church. Most important, people in this country perceive churches and synagogues today as being overly engaged in organizational matters. Fifty-nine percent of adults think that churches and synagogues should turn their focus away from matters of administration and organization and concentrate more intently on theological and spiritual matters. Between the 1970s and 1990s, this concern expressed by Americans has increased by eight percentage points from 51% in 1978 to 59% just ten years later. Second, Americans express a concern that places of worship are not as interested in social justice issues as they need to be. Over four in ten (41%) adults agree that organized religion is not concerned enough with this sector of society. This percentage has also risen since 1978 (from 35%) to the present

Organized Religion Takes Its Test

Would you tell me after each [statement] whether you strongly agree, moderately agree, are uncertain, moderately disagree, or strongly disagree?

	STRONGLY AGREE	MODERATELY AGREE	UNCERTAIN	STRONGLY DISAGREE	DON'T KNOW
Most churches and synagogues today have a clear sense of the real spiritual nature of religion.	48%	32%	8%	8%	4%
The rules about morality preached by the churches and synagogues today are too restrictive.	9%	23%	22%	28%	18%
Most churches and synagogues today are warm and accepting of outsiders.	24%	40%	19%	12%	5%
Most churches and synagogues today are too concerned with organizational, as opposed to theological or spiritual, issues.	24%	35%	25%	13%	3%
Most churches and synagogues today are not concerned enough with social justice.	14%	27%	30%	22%	7%
Most churches and synagogues today are effective in helping people find meaning in life.	22%	45%	18%	11%	4%

Source: Gallup Survey on the "Unchurched American," 1988

figure. Third, a fairly even split exists within the populace regarding the restrictive morality preached by religious bodies. Approximately the same number of people who feel that the church's morality is too restrictive suggest that it is not. The increases relating to the church's overzealous interest in organizational matters and overly restrictive preaching are greater among churched Americans than unchurched respondents.

The American people also have words of affirmation regarding today's churches and synagogues. Eight out of ten adults think that the religious bodies in this country have a clear sense of the real spiritual nature of religion. Two out of three people in this country (67%) think that organized religion successfully leads people in finding meaning for their lives. Finally, churches and synagogues also score high on welcoming outsiders. Over six in ten adults (64%) agree that places of worship are warm and accepting of outsiders. Those on the "outside" of the church, the unchurched, agree far less than churchgoers on the church's hospitality to outsiders, by a margin of 53% to 73%. Blacks are slightly more likely than Whites to agree, by 69% to 66%.

SMALL GROUPS

Small group activity in American life exerts pervasive influence in the lives of over 100 million Americans every year. With 40% of the adult population participating in some type of regular small group meeting, both ecclesial and secular organizations are increasingly using small groups as a means to combat the fragmentation that occurs in today's society. The church has incorporated the splintering of society into small groups in order to create opportunities for greater pastoral care and spiritual support. Both church attenders and members participate in regular small groups with greater frequency than the general population (62% and 52%, respectively). More Protestants than Catholics participate in small groups, and over six in ten born-again believers meet in some type of small group on a regular basis. The greatest amount of commitment appears among those Americans who regard religion as extremely important in their own lives (65%).

For many small group members participation is anything but casual, with about two in three reporting they are attending group gatherings at least twice a month (63%), that the meetings are lasting an hour or more (65%), and that they have been doing this for three or more years (64%). Although groups tend to attract more women than men and to appeal to older adults and to those who are better educated, these and other demographic differences are only slight. Small group membership is a phenomenon that embraces people from all walks of life, in all regions of the country, and in communities of every size.

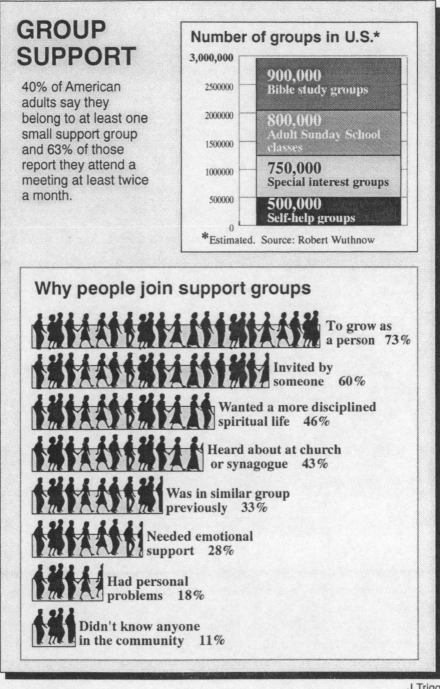

GROUP SUPPORT

40% of American adults say they belong to at least one small support group and 63% of those report they attend a meeting at least twice a month.

Number of groups in U.S.*

- **900,000** Bible study groups
- **800,000** Adult Sunday School classes
- **750,000** Special interest groups
- **500,000** Self-help groups

*Estimated. Source: Robert Wuthnow

Why people join support groups

To grow as a person **73%**

Invited by someone **60%**

Wanted a more disciplined spiritual life **46%**

Heard about at church or synagogue **43%**

Was in similar group previously **33%**

Needed emotional support **28%**

Had personal problems **18%**

Didn't know anyone in the community **11%**

J. Trigg

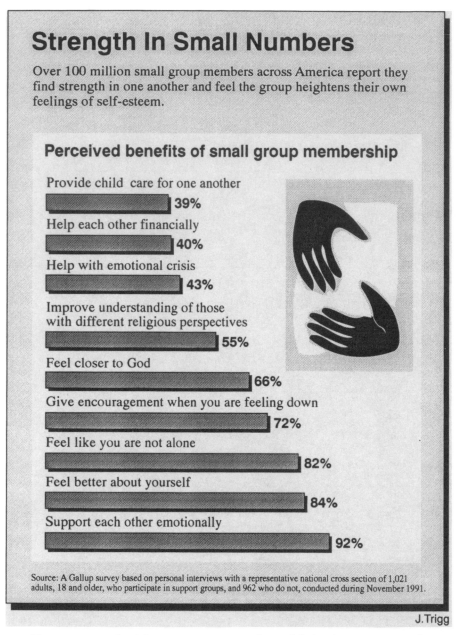

Strength In Small Numbers

Over 100 million small group members across America report they find strength in one another and feel the group heightens their own feelings of self-esteem.

Perceived benefits of small group membership

Provide child care for one another
39%

Help each other financially
40%

Help with emotional crisis
43%

Improve understanding of those with different religious perspectives
55%

Feel closer to God
66%

Give encouragement when you are feeling down
72%

Feel like you are not alone
82%

Feel better about yourself
84%

Support each other emotionally
92%

Source: A Gallup survey based on personal interviews with a representative national cross section of 1,021 adults, 18 and older, who participate in support groups, and 962 who do not, conducted during November 1991.

J.Trigg

Encounter and crisis groups generate the publicity, but most people say they joined support groups for more general reasons, such as desiring personal growth, being invited by a friend, seeking a more structured spiritual life, or simply because it became known to them through their place of worship. One member in three joined because of a previous rewarding experience in a similar group.

The German Pietist movement during the seventeenth century encouraged believers to meet together in small group "conventicles" or "colleges of piety" for consistent spiritual growth and edification. Likewise, John and Charles Wesley and other members of the "Holy Club" at Oxford met regularly

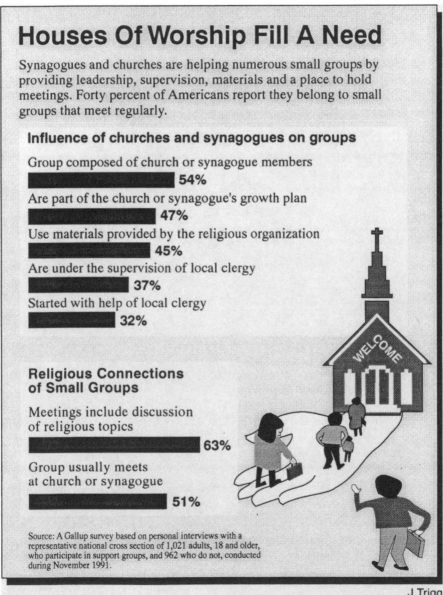

Houses Of Worship Fill A Need

Synagogues and churches are helping numerous small groups by providing leadership, supervision, materials and a place to hold meetings. Forty percent of Americans report they belong to small groups that meet regularly.

Influence of churches and synagogues on groups

Group composed of church or synagogue members
54%

Are part of the church or synagogue's growth plan
47%

Use materials provided by the religious organization
45%

Are under the supervision of local clergy
37%

Started with help of local clergy
32%

Religious Connections of Small Groups

Meetings include discussion of religious topics
63%

Group usually meets at church or synagogue
51%

Source: A Gallup survey based on personal interviews with a representative national cross section of 1,021 adults, 18 and older, who participate in support groups, and 962 who do not, conducted during November 1991.

J. Trigg

Widespread Commitment to Small Groups of Faith

Members of America's small groups were asked about the following spiritual aspects of their gatherings:

	PERCENTAGE OF GROUP MEMBERS
Belongs to a religious congregation that encourages small group participation	71%
Group meetings include praying together	69%
Meetings include discussion of religious topics	63%
Meeting is a part of the regular activities of the religious congregation	57%
Group meetings include the study or discussion of Scripture	56%
Group usually meets at church or synagogue	51%
At least half of the member's congregation is involved in small groups	38%

Source: George H. Gallup International Institute with support by a grant from the Lilly Endowment, 1994

for prayer, Bible study, and spiritual accountability. Small groups with religious interests are not a new phenomenon, but the current popularity of these gatherings is historically unprecedented. More people of faith meet today in small groups than ever before.

Seven in ten small group members (71%) report they are also members of a religious congregation that encourages small group participation. Over a third endorse their congregation's success in getting those on the church rolls to participate in small group activities. A majority of 57% characterize small groups as a regular activity of their church or synagogue, and half say the local house of worship is where they usually meet. Given this setting, it is not surprising that many small groups pray together (69%), consider and examine religious topics (63%), and study or discuss the Bible (56%).

Recent findings underscore the strong spiritual influence of many groups by noting that two members in three of all groups—not just those that are church-related—say their groups lead them closer to God. Fifty-seven percent profess that the Bible has become more meaningful to them as a result of their group experience. Over half the members also believe their involvement, rather than fostering insular or parochial religious practices, has given them a better understanding of people with religious perspectives different from their own (55%) as well as spurred them to serve others outside the group (55%). Many in groups pray together, and 54% say their prayers have been answered.

On a more personal level, groups clearly offer support to many of their members, with 82% saying the small groups dispel feelings of loneliness and separation in our increasingly splintering society. Seventy-two percent report that small groups provide much-needed encouragement during times of despair and loss. Groups help people during good and bad times, helping people celebrate (51%), handle emotional crises (43%), make decisions (38%), and receive assistance during times of sickness (38%).

"UNCHURCHED" AMERICA

Gallup findings on the percentage of Americans in this country who are classified as "unchurched" are based on two primary questions that have been asked over the past three decades. First, Gallup asks respondents, "Are you, yourself, a member of a church or synagogue?" The second question is then asked: "Apart from weddings, funerals, or special holidays such as Christmas, Easter, or Yom Kippur, have you attended the church or synagogue of your choice in the past six months, or not?" In order for an individual to be regarded as "churched" for Gallup research, the person must respond affirmatively to both questions. All others—meaning those who answer negatively to either or both questions—are considered to be "unchurched." Gallup has employed this working definition, albeit one open to some degree of criticism considering the nuances of these types of categories, for all of the surveys on this topic conducted over the last three decades. As a result, the consistency of the questions lends credence to the research and substantiates the validity of the results.

The percentage of Americans who are "unchurched"—that is, who are without a church membership or who have not attended regular services within the last six months—has changed little over the last two decades. In a recent Gallup study, 44% of Americans are classified as "unchurched," the same figure as recorded a decade earlier in 1988, and only slightly higher than the percentage recorded in 1978 (41%).

While the trend shows no gain for organized religion over the last twenty years, it could be maintained that churches and other faith communities have had some measure of success in keeping slippage at a minimum given the continued high mobility of Americans, the distractions of modern life, and

"Unchurched" America Has Changed Little in 20 Years

UNCHURCHED

Demographic profile of the "unchurched."
Note: The unchurched are defined as those who are not members of a church or have not attended services in the previous six months other than for special religious holidays, weddings, funerals, or the like.

	Percentage of people who are "unchurched"
National	44%
Male	50%
Female	39%
Whites	45%
Non-Whites	37%
Blacks	32%
18–29 years	49%
30–49 years	44%
50–64 years	42%
65+	40%
East	47%
Midwest	41%
South	39%
West	52%
College	40%
High School or Less	49%
Conservatives	35%
Moderates	47%
Liberals	55%
1998	44%
1988	44%
1978	41%

Source: The Gallup Poll, 1998

the appeal of nontraditional religious movements. In general, the unchurched are more likely to be men (50% compared with 39% of women) and under 30 years old (49%). Moreover, people living in the West have a greater propensity to be unchurched; 52% of the population there falls into this category. People living in the South as well as those who live in rural environments are more apt to either be members of a church or attend a religious service aside from special occasions.

Race represents one of the areas of sharpest divergence on the matter of church participation. Almost one in two Whites (45%) are classified as unchurched, but the figure drops to below one in three (32%) among Blacks in this country. However, the greatest distinction appears among ideological subcultures of the American population. Whereas 55% of liberals in this country dissociate themselves from a church, only 35% of conservatives fall into the same category.

Religion and Ethics

Throughout human history religion has been used as a crutch and a club for divergent ethical responses. Adherents have justified everything from the divine right of kings to popular democracy. Within this country, individuals have employed religious dogma to conclusively settle matters such as slavery and segregation, prohibition and pacifism, and on many topics, people have later renounced these conclusions again on spiritual grounds.

Regardless of creedal affiliations, U.S. adults decry dishonesty and flagging moral standards prevalent in contemporary society. Nearly eight in ten Americans pronounce their dissatisfaction with the ethical climate of this nation. Scandals that plague the presidency and other cultural leaders further exacerbate the moral malaise felt by many Americans. Between the 1960s and the 1990s, disapproval of the state of America's morality has climbed twenty percentage points, and millions of adults in this country increasingly speak of a state of moral ennui that permeates many sectors of the general population.

Abortion ranks as the top moral dilemma of the last three decades of the twentieth century. Both pro-choice and pro-life advocates appeal to religious ideals in their conflicting responses to the abortion debate. Violent responses, such as the murder of members of the opposing camp, committed by extremist radicals, further alienate the two groups from each other. Since the Supreme Court's historic decision in *Roe v. Wade* (1973), opinions on the matter have remained largely unchanged with one exception. Americans today are less likely than they were in 1973 to pronounce abortion illegal in *all* circumstances. Even among pro-life advocates, allowances are made for abortions being performed in unusual circumstances. When the woman's life is endangered, for instance, 88% of the population affirms the legality of an abortion. However, the approval rating drops to its lowest level (32%) when a woman chooses abortion simply because she or the family cannot afford the baby.

A majority of Americans fear that moral values in our society will be worse in 2025 than they are today. Over three in five adults express this concern, and Americans rank church and religious leaders as doing the best job currently to help counteract the declining morality of our society. With 36% of the nation thinking that ministers currently do a good job, almost seven in ten adults (68%) affirm the prospect of religious leaders exerting an even greater influence in reinvigorating American morality.

Opinions on premarital sex and physician-assisted suicide emerge largely from religious convictions. Many who regard religion as important in their lives reject sex outside of marriage as immoral and sinful. Almost all older Americans who endorse religious belief condemn premarital sex. By contrast, only one in four young people (ages 18 to 29) deem premarital sex as wrong. Similarly, those most opposed to legalization of physician-assisted suicide are persons who rank faith as very important to their lives. Sixty-eight percent of these Americans renounce the practice of euthanasia. Also, one-half of born-again people in this country reject its legalization; only 19% of those who do not describe themselves this way hold the same opinion.

Michelangelo chiseled and toiled for four years on his famous statue of David, which is now housed in Florence, Italy. His task was especially arduous because he was working with a piece of flawed marble. The block had been damaged when it was removed from the quarry. We remember that David, too, was flawed. Since ancient times, people have struggled with the tension between exalting their leaders while recognizing their humanity. Americans today continue to grapple with this issue. Moral dilemmas came to the forefront of public concern in 1998 with President Bill Clinton's admission of an "inappropriate relationship" with White House intern Monica Lewinsky. Americans have long esteemed propriety and moral behavior for their national leaders. We recall that one of the contributing factors to Gary Hart's demise as a presidential hopeful in 1988 was his extramarital relationship with Donna Rice. Just ten years later, a number of Americans called for President Clinton's resignation after hearing the disappointing news of his extramarital relationship. Seventy-nine percent of Americans reject extramarital sexual relations as unacceptable and inappropriate.

Prior to President Clinton's admission, 65% of the American people ranked the president's responsibility of providing moral leadership for the country as very important. Seven months later, in September 1998, that number had jumped seven percentage points, which reflects statistically significant change in such a short span of time. At the same time, three out of four Americans rated the moral values of this country "somewhat weak" or "very weak." Nearly half of the population (49%) viewed the president's impropriety as a "moral crisis" for the entire nation.

Although a relationship between religion and ethics clearly can be seen in the American context, most Americans consider the two realms distinct from each other. Three-fourths of the country believe that a person can be ethical without faith in God. An even higher percentage of young adults (ages 18 to 29) suppose that atheists can live moral, ethical lives. Since only a small slice of the population claims to be atheist (5%), this issue deals much more with the realm of possibility than it does reality.

The ethics of the death penalty represents one moral area where religious conviction exerts surprising influence. Although most religious Americans marshal support in favor of human life on matters such as abortion and euthanasia, most religious adherents favor capital punishment (84%) for convicted murderers. Only 10% of them oppose capital punishment. The death penalty is gaining favor across the United States. A higher percentage of Americans in the 1990s favor the death penalty than they did in the 1950s, 1960s, and 1970s, although support declines when conditional statements—for example, the option of life without parole—are added to the basic question.

In summary, most people in this country regret the demise of moral values that they observe in today's society. From the entertainment industry to the sensationalized scandals that entangle popular culture icons, politicians, and local heroes, Americans are surrounded by a culture that breaks many of society's mores to the disapproval of most citizens. Two centuries ago President George Washington said, "And let us with caution indulge the supposition that morality can be maintained without religion.... Reason and experience both forbid us to expect that National morality can prevail in exclusion of religious principle."[18] Many Americans believe morality's foundation is religion. Moral choices on abortion, premarital sex, euthanasia, and the death penalty embroil masses of the American population in ethical dilemmas, and many of them rely upon religious convictions to help settle the matter. Furthermore, Gallup research shows that a majority of Americans (68%) consider church and religious leaders as the greatest bastion of hope against the further encroachment of moral failure for this nation in the coming millennium.

HONESTY AND ETHICS

Public opinion regarding the honesty and standards of behavior among Americans sank to its lowest level for three decades in 1992. In fact, the last time the American people expressed such dissatisfaction with the honesty of their fellow citizens was 1973, the year of the Watergate hearings. In the 1980s and the 1960s, one in three U.S. adults considered the nation's standards of behavior acceptable. Although this reflects a minority of the population, these were the highest percentages in the history of Gallup's research. Gallup surveys in 1992 reveal that only one in five adults is satisfied with the honesty and standards of behavior in this country.

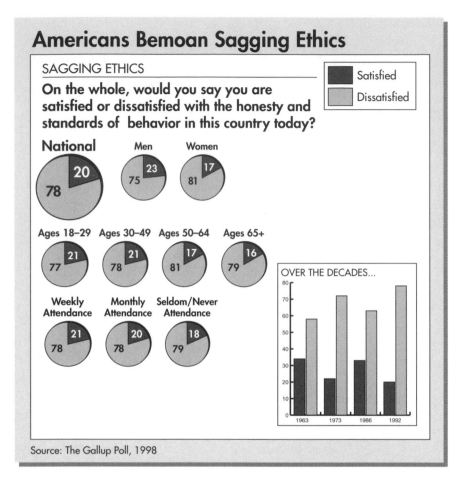

Americans Bemoan Sagging Ethics

SAGGING ETHICS

On the whole, would you say you are satisfied or dissatisfied with the honesty and standards of behavior in this country today?

■ Satisfied
□ Dissatisfied

National — 20 / 78

Men — 23 / 75

Women — 17 / 81

Ages 18–29 — 21 / 77

Ages 30–49 — 21 / 78

Ages 50–64 — 17 / 81

Ages 65+ — 16 / 79

Weekly Attendance — 21 / 78

Monthly Attendance — 20 / 78

Seldom/Never Attendance — 18 / 79

OVER THE DECADES...

1963 1973 1986 1992

Source: The Gallup Poll, 1998

Gallup research shows that every subsection of the American population is dissatisfied with the honesty and the ethical behavior of people in this country. The highest level of satisfaction to be found within all of the demographic groups comes from Americans earning more than $50,000 income each year. Even within this group, the figure remains a paltry 24%. It is reasonable to conclude, therefore, that strong dissatisfaction can be found across all racial, gender, ethnic, political, religious, economic, and ideological boundaries. Although overwhelming majorities in all major sectors of the population show discontent with the current ethical climate in the United States, somewhat greater concern appears among Blacks, women, and Protestants. Dissatisfaction among those who attend church—either on a weekly or monthly basis—mirrors the discontent expressed among the general population.

PREMARITAL SEX

Two in five adults think it is wrong for a man and a woman to have sexual relations before marriage. This follows a general trend between 1969 and 1996 in which more and more Americans approved of premarital sex. Pope Paul VI's encyclical, *Humanae Vitae*, brought the discussion of human sexual mores to the modern religious context. In this papal decree, the Roman Catholic Church commented on human sexuality and upheld the Church's traditional ban on artificial means of birth control. Since then, Americans of all faith groups have moved further away from this perspective held by the Church, and they have shown increasing approval of sex before marriage. In 1969 nearly seven out of ten adults considered sexual relations prior to marriage inappropriate. That figure fell below the 50% mark by 1973. That year 48% of the American people said that sex before marriage was wrong. Since then, more and more Americans say they think that sexual relations before marriage are acceptable. By 1996 the percentage of Americans who viewed premarital sex as wrong dropped by a remarkable twenty-nine percentage points, from 68% in the 1969 survey to 39% in 1996.

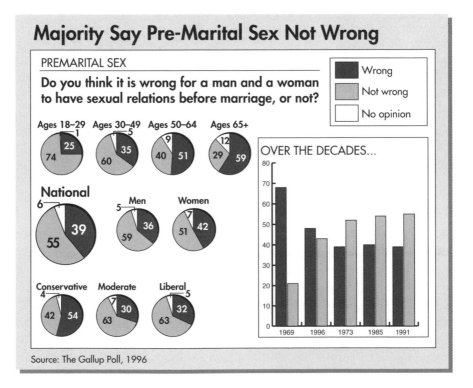

Source: The Gallup Poll, 1996

A Gallup study in 1996 shows that women are more likely to object to premarital sex than men (42% of women compared with 36% of men). College-educated men are most likely to say that sex prior to marriage is acceptable; 65% of them condone premarital sex. Americans who claim a conservative ideology are more likely to disapprove of premarital sex. Fifty-four percent of conservatives disapprove of sex before marriage, whereas only 32% of liberals hold the same view.

The greatest distinction, however, can be seen among different age groups of the American population. An overwhelming majority of young people, ages 18 to 29, think that sex before marriage is allowable (74%). This is the strongest amount of approval found among any of the subcategories of the American people. Only 25% of American young people deem premarital sex as wrong. Their older counterparts, however, disagree. Among adults who are 50 to 64 years old, 51% disagree with sex before marriage. The percentage jumps to 59% among adults over the age of 65. In summary, forty-five percentage points separate the approval of premarital sex for adults who are 18 to 29 years old and those over age 65—a noteworthy difference. In other words, the difference in opinion between today's young adults and senior adults is greater than the difference in opinion expressed on the national level between 1969 and 1996.

Americans show much greater resistance to endorsing sex *outside* marriage. In a related Gallup study, a majority of Americans disapprove of extramarital sexual relations. Consistently over the last quarter of the twentieth century, large majorities have said that it is "always wrong" for a married person to have sexual relations with someone other than their marriage partner.[19] While a number of studies on adultery show that it is not uncommon, the Gallup findings on attitudes toward adultery indicate that for the vast majority of people (79% in 1997) such behavior is still unacceptable and inappropriate.

ABORTION

Abortion may be the hottest debate in the American political arena over the last three decades. It is certainly the most intense topic in the political realm that has strong affiliation with religious beliefs. It is interesting to see, however, that public opinion regarding abortion has changed little at the national level since the Supreme Court's 1973 landmark decision upholding a woman's right to have an abortion. Gallup research shows that one of the most distinguishing differences in opinion between the late 1990s and the 1970s relates to absolutes on the matter; that is, fewer people support absolute legality or illegality in all circumstances. In 1975, for example, 22% of American adults

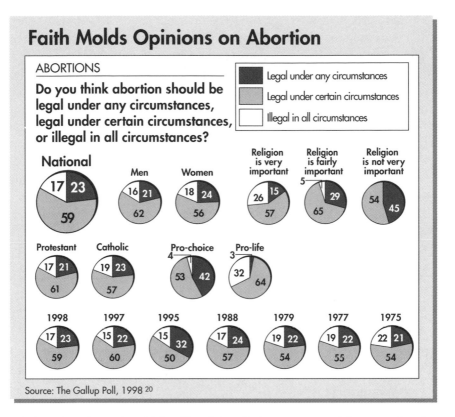

Faith Molds Opinions on Abortion

ABORTIONS

Do you think abortion should be legal under any circumstances, legal under certain circumstances, or illegal in all circumstances?

- ■ Legal under any circumstances
- ▨ Legal under certain circumstances
- □ Illegal in all circumstances

Source: The Gallup Poll, 1998 [20]

said that abortions should be illegal in all circumstances. That number has dwindled since 1975 among all demographic groups of the population; in 1998 only 17% hold this belief. Although this represents a drop of only five percentage points, the difference has been consistent for over a decade and thus suggests a genuine change of opinion. Moreover, on the national level, it is one of the primary trends that can be seen clearly over the three decades of Gallup research.

In 1973 the Supreme Court ruled that states could not place restrictions on a woman's right to an abortion during the first three months of pregnancy. In the second trimester, the states have no authority to prevent an abortion but can regulate certain areas of the medical aspects involved. Only during the final trimester, when medical experts generally agree that the fetus is capable of living outside the womb, can states impose restrictions on a woman's right to an abortion.

The 1998 survey shows some interesting distinctions among different groups of the American population. Women, for example, are more likely than men (18% compared to 16%) to believe that abortions should be illegal in all circumstances. Democrats and wealthy Americans are more supportive of allowing abortions in any circumstances. The greatest disapproval for abortions comes from people who regard religion as "very important" in their lives. Twenty-six percent of them say that abortions should be illegal in all circumstances. This stands in sharp contrast to those who say religion is "not very important." Among these individuals, less than one half of one percent said that abortions should be illegal in all circumstances. Beliefs on abortions among Catholics and Protestants mirror each other.

A summary of all Gallup research regarding abortions over the last three decades of the twentieth century highlights one clear trend: the majority of

Many Approve of Abortions in Special Situations

Please tell me whether you think abortions should or should not be legal under each of the following circumstances:

	SHOULD BE LEGAL	SHOULD BE ILLEGAL	DEPENDS
Woman's life is endangered	88%	7%	3%
Rape or incest	77%	18%	3%
Woman's physical health is endangered	82%	11%	5%
Woman's mental health is endangered	66%	27%	5%
Baby may be physically impaired	53%	37%	7%
Baby may be mentally impaired	54%	36%	7%
Cannot afford child	32%	62%	3%

Source: The Gallup Poll, 1996

Americans—regardless of ideology, religious belief, or political affiliation—believe that abortions should be legal under certain circumstances.

Because most Americans believe that abortions should be legal in certain circumstances, Gallup polled public opinion on abortion under specific conditions. The greatest amount of support for the legality of abortion occurs when the woman's life is endangered by the pregnancy. However, Gallup findings reveal that Americans hold conflicting opinions. For example, a majority of 56% of those Americans who claim to believe that abortions should be illegal in all circumstances still support an abortion when the woman's life is endangered. College-educated men offer the most support for abortions in this situation (92%). Blacks and pro-life citizens express the most disapproval of abortion for the sake of the mother's life.

Furthermore, Americans are much more likely to approve of abortion when the woman's physical health is endangered than when the woman's mental health is endangered (82% versus 66%). Americans reject abortions done solely on economic grounds. Only one in three Americans approve of abortion when performed because the woman or family cannot afford to raise the child. Even among abortion supporters, this last circumstance has little approval. Only 36% of Democrats affirm aborting a baby because the family cannot afford the child. Just over half (55%) of liberals would allow abortion in this situation. Surprisingly, even the most ardent abortion supporters express disapproval of this reason for performing an abortion. Twenty-two percent of those adults who claim to believe that abortions should be legal in all circumstances still say that an abortion should not be allowed if performed solely because the family cannot afford the child. It appears that some abortion rights activists waver in their convictions when pressed to make a decision in this specific circumstance. Indeed, two pro-choice citizens out of five think that abortions for economic reasons should be illegal.

Presidential Ethics

In 1994, 83% of Americans believed that personal and moral values were the most important qualities for a future president to possess. In assessing these personal and moral attributes, 37% of those who hold this belief rank "personal honesty" as the most important personal attribute for a future president. In addition, sizable numbers of people value "high ethics" (34%) and "strong religious faith" (13%) for a future president of this country. Older Americans are more likely to esteem personal and moral values in a presidential candidate than are younger people. In addition, this factor is more important to people in this country with lower incomes and those living in rural or farm areas. In terms of skills and abilities, "sound judgment" (42%) is named

Eight out of Ten Value Morals in Presidential Hopefuls

Which quality is most important for a future president?

Personal and moral values	83%
Skills and abilities	69%
Previous experience	44%
Political style	26%

Source: George H. Gallup International Institute, Survey for William Moss, 1994

Do you feel a person must have strong moral values in order to be an effective president, or can someone be an effective president regardless of their moral values?

Must have strong moral values	61%
No, can be effective regardless	37%
Don't know/Refused	2%

Source: The Gallup Poll, 1998

When it comes to the moral standards of our presidents, do you think American presidents are held to a higher standard or a lower standard than they were in the past?

Higher standard	63%
Lower standard	29%
Same standard/No charge	5%
Don't know/Refused	3%

Source: The Gallup Poll, 1998

ahead of "leadership" (30%) with "good communication skills" (13%) or "high intelligence" (9%) lagging far behind.

The president's morality came to the forefront of the discussion in 1998 when President Bill Clinton's "inappropriate relationship" with White House intern Monica Lewinsky topped news stories. During that year, 61% of American adults said that an effective president must have strong moral values. A sizable portion of the population (37%) disagreed. A little bit more consensus was found on the question of today's standards for the president. Sixty-three percent of the people in this country think that presidents today are held to a higher standard of behavior than previous presidents.

Gallup research indicates a change in public opinion regarding the president's responsibility as a moral leader in 1998. Prior to President Bill Clinton's admission of an "improper relationship" on August 17, 1998, 65% of Americans said that it is "very important" that the president provide moral leadership for the nation. By September, that figure had risen to 72%. In both cases, an overwhelming majority of Americans ranked moral leadership as "very" or "somewhat important" for the president of the United States to provide. The president's behavior also appears to run counter to most Americans' opinion on extramarital relations. Related Gallup studies show that an overwhelming majority of Americans (79%) disapprove of adultery, saying that it is "always wrong" for a married person to have sexual relations with someone other than their marriage partner.

In 1998 a substantial plurality of Americans also decried this nation's morals as "somewhat weak." Another 34% of the population called them "very weak." Only one in four Americans (24%) declared the nation's morals to be "very" or "somewhat strong." Similarly, nearly one-half (49%) of Americans expressed concern that a moral crisis currently grips the United States. An additional 41% noted that there are major problems with regards to morality in the United States. Furthermore, fewer than one in ten (8%) Americans believe that moral conditions are not a major problem for this nation.

In the midst of a moral crisis, nearly one in three adults (29%) considers moral values in the United States as "extremely important." Even more Americans (36%) regard moral values as "very important." Another quarter of the population (24%) say that moral values are "somewhat important." The remaining 11% of adults said that morals are not important or that they did not know.

Millennial Morality

Americans are twice as likely as not (62% compared to 31%) to believe that the moral values of society will be worse in 2025 than they are today. Given

Morality Increasingly Important for U.S. Presidents

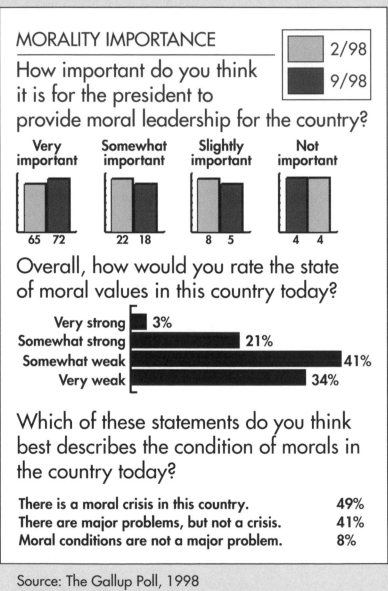

MORALITY IMPORTANCE

2/98
9/98

How important do you think it is for the president to provide moral leadership for the country?

Very important	Somewhat important	Slightly important	Not important
65 72	22 18	8 5	4 4

Overall, how would you rate the state of moral values in this country today?

Very strong — 3%
Somewhat strong — 21%
Somewhat weak — 41%
Very weak — 34%

Which of these statements do you think best describes the condition of morals in the country today?

There is a moral crisis in this country.	49%
There are major problems, but not a crisis.	41%
Moral conditions are not a major problem.	8%

Source: The Gallup Poll, 1998

this staggering statistic, many Americans express a hope for various institutions in society to provide greater moral leadership. Currently, church and religious leaders lead the list for doing a good job at raising the moral and ethical standards for contemporary culture. One in three adults (36%) praise

Millennial Morality

For each of the following, please say whether you expect conditions in this area to be better or worse in the year 2025 than they are today. How about moral values in society?

Better	31%
Worse	62%
Same	5%
Don't know/Refused	3%

Source: The Gallup Poll, 1998

What kind of a job do you think the following have been doing in raising the moral and ethical standards of the nation? Would you say a good job, a fair job, or a poor job? Regardless of the kind of job you think these have been doing, how much influence do you think each *could* have on raising the moral and ethical standards of the nation? Would you say a great deal, some, or not much influence?

INSTITUTIONS	NOW DOING A GOOD JOB	COULD HAVE A GREAT DEAL OF INFLUENCE
Church or religious leaders	36%	68%
Recent presidents	13%	68%
Newspapers	13%	59%
Advertising	12%	60%
Example of individual role models in the news	11%	56%
Big business	11%	49%
Movies	5%	60%
Television	5%	78%
Congress	5%	54%

Source: George H. Gallup International Institute, Survey for William Moss, 1994

church and religious leaders for doing a good job. Americans ranked recent presidents and newspapers as a distant second (13%). Advertising, individuals in the news, and big business lagged behind them (12%, 11%, and 11%, respectively). Only one in twenty people in this country (5%) deem movies, television, or Congress as doing a good job at lifting the national standard of morality.

Overall, Americans believe that all of these institutions have the potential to exert tremendous influence on society's morality and ethics. In the area of television, adults showed the greatest distinction between the institution's present performance and the potential for it to do a good job in the future. An astonishing 73 percentage points separated these two issues; whereas only 5% of the population thinks that television is doing a good job today, 78% think that it has the *potential* to do a good job at raising the nation's standards of morality. Another sector of the entertainment industry, movies, also ranks near the top in terms of difference between what the institution could be doing and what it currently does. Fifty-five percentage points separate the two issues (5% versus 60%). By the same point spread, Americans think that recent presidents could exert more influence; although only 13% of the population thinks that recent presidents are currently doing a good job, 68% of them think that recent presidents could use their position to exercise greater influence in remedying the moral malaise of this country.

ETHICS WITHOUT GOD

Nationwide, three persons in four (74%) judge that a person can live an ethical life without a belief in God. Atheists and agnostics constitute a very small section of the American population; only about 5% of the adults in this country allege to hold a complete lack of belief in God or at least seriously doubt their ability to know whether God or a supreme being exists. This national trend regarding ethics and atheists appears throughout almost every subculture of the population.

Among both men and women, a strong majority affirm the possibility of an atheist living an ethical life. Women do, however, hesitate a little more than men do, but still seven in ten American women think that a person can live ethically without subscribing to a belief in God or a supreme being. Slight differences of opinion also surface between the younger and older members of our society. Ten percentage points separate the two groups: 18% of young people think a person cannot live a good and ethical life without a belief in God, and 28% of older people surmise the same. Slim margins of difference exist between Protestants and Roman Catholics on the issue.

Ethics Do Not Hinge Upon Religious Faith

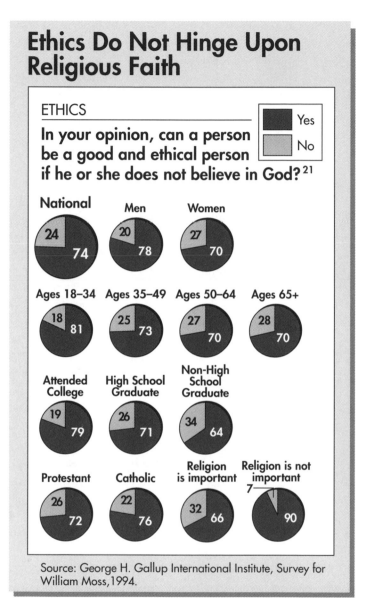

ETHICS

In your opinion, can a person be a good and ethical person if he or she does not believe in God? [21]

Yes
No

Source: George H. Gallup International Institute, Survey for William Moss, 1994.

Interestingly, political party preference has little influence upon people's opinions on the matter.

People who consider religion to be very important in their lives express the greatest doubts about the ability of atheists to lead virtuous lives. Nearly one in three (32%) of these religious adherents dissent from the prevailing national opinion on this matter. Still, a majority of those who deem religion important in their lives (66%) affirm the prospect of atheists practicing ethical and moral lives. Americans who do not value religion as important offer the greatest margin of approval for atheists living in an upright manner. Nine out of ten of these people say that a person who does not believe in God or a supreme being can live a good and ethical life. Only 7% of this group conclude that an atheist cannot live ethically.

PHYSICIAN-ASSISTED SUICIDE

The activities of Dr. Jack Kevorkian in Michigan have sparked national interest in the practice of physician-assisted suicide. In June 1997 the Supreme Court upheld state laws that prohibit assisted suicide. In late 1998, the CBS news-magazine show, *60 Minutes*, played a videotape that Dr. Kevorkian made of himself while participating in the suicide of one of his patients. Many people challenged the network's judgment and motive in showing this video, particularly since the segment was shown during the annual ratings season for network television. Almost two-thirds of the American people, however, support legalizing physician-assisted suicide in some form: 33% supporting its legalization "under a wide variety of specific" circumstances and 32% supporting its legalization "in a few cases." Close to another third of the nation (31%) oppose legalization "for any reason." The three-way split in opinions about legalizing physician-assisted suicide became a fifty-fifty split when the respondents were asked about how they felt about the possibility for themselves.

Spiritual beliefs are strongly linked to attitudes on physician-assisted suicide. Most opposed to legalization are persons who place the highest importance on their religious faith as an influence in their lives, who say their life belongs to God or a Higher Power rather than to themselves, their families, or the communities around them. Sixty-eight percent of those who say that their religious faith is the most important influence in their lives reject legalizing physician-assisted suicide. Yet only 11% of those for whom faith is not an important influence hold the same opinion. Similarly, 46% of those who believe their life belongs to God or a Higher Power oppose legalization while only 13% who say their lives belong to themselves believe the same. Fifty percent of those who describe themselves as born again reject making physician-assisted suicide legal for any reason, compared to 19% of those who do not describe themselves in those terms.

Significant differences of opinion also surface between those who do and do not believe in heaven and/or hell. Further, distinctions appear—although not so dramatic—between those with varying opinions on existence in some

Public Split on Physician-Assisted Suicide

There has been a lot in the news about physician-assisted suicide and whether or not it should be legal. Which of these statements comes closest to your own views on legalizing physician-assisted suicide?

	NATIONAL RESULTS
You support making it legal under a wide variety of specific circumstances.	33%
You support making it legal in a few cases but oppose it in most circumstances.	32%
You oppose making it legal for any reason.	31%
Don't know/Refused	4%

Can you imagine any situation where you yourself might want your doctor to end your life intentionally by some painless means if you requested it?

Can imagine such a situation	50%
Cannot imagine such a situation	47%
Don't know/Refused	3%

Source: The Gallup Institute for Nathan Cummings Foundation and Fetzer Institute, 1997

form following death. For example, those who presume that they will exist in some form after death are more likely to oppose legalization for any reason. These same people cannot imagine applying physician-assisted suicide to themselves. Among those who believe in some form of after-death existence, those who say that their faith or beliefs lead them to this conviction are even more likely to oppose legalization and to say that they cannot imagine physician-assisted suicide for themselves.

Differences in age and racial/ethnic background bear some relationship to attitudes on this matter. Younger adults are more inclined to support legalizing assisted suicide than those who are age 55 or older (37% for those ages 18 to 34, for example, compared to 28% for those age 65 or older). Those younger than age 55 are also more liable than are those who are older than 55 to imagine a situation where they might want to have their doctor end their life (53% for those ages 18 to 34 versus only 35% for those age 65 or older). Whites are more likely than minority groups to support legalization and much more likely than minority groups to imagine a situation in which they would support physician-assisted suicide for themselves (53% of Whites versus 39% of non-Whites).

CAPITAL PUNISHMENT

The American public supports the death penalty for those convicted of murder. A strong majority (77%) of adults favor its use in punishing murderers

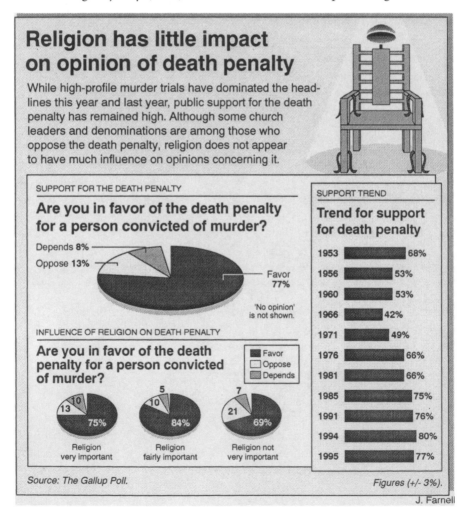

Religion has little impact on opinion of death penalty

While high-profile murder trials have dominated the headlines this year and last year, public support for the death penalty has remained high. Although some church leaders and denominations are among those who oppose the death penalty, religion does not appear to have much influence on opinions concerning it.

SUPPORT FOR THE DEATH PENALTY

Are you in favor of the death penalty for a person convicted of murder?

Depends 8%
Oppose 13%
Favor 77%

'No opinion' is not shown.

INFLUENCE OF RELIGION ON DEATH PENALTY

Are you in favor of the death penalty for a person convicted of murder?

Favor
Oppose
Depends

Religion very important — 13, 10, 75%
Religion fairly important — 10, 5, 84%
Religion not very important — 21, 7, 69%

SUPPORT TREND

Trend for support for death penalty

Year	Support
1953	68%
1956	53%
1960	53%
1966	42%
1971	49%
1976	66%
1981	66%
1985	75%
1991	76%
1994	80%
1995	77%

Source: The Gallup Poll.

Figures (+/- 3%).

J. Farnell

in this country. Support for the death penalty climaxed in 1994 when 80% of the public voiced their approval. Support ebbed to its lowest level in 1966 when just 42% of Americans approved of the penalty, with a plurality of 47% opposed to it.

Even though 82% of the population suspects that at least some people have been wrongfully executed for murders they did not commit, they still endorse the death penalty. When informed that experts estimate that one person in one hundred who is condemned to death is innocent, the public by a two-to-one margin continues to support its use. In other words, when told that 1% of the time the death penalty is used to punish a person who is, indeed, innocent, 57% still support the death penalty compared with 28% who do not endorse it given this information.

Although some church leaders and denominations are in the vanguard of those who oppose the death penalty, religion does not appear to have much influence upon opinions concerning it. Indeed, opposition to imposing the death penalty is most likely to arise from people who say religion is not very important in their lives. This statistic changed in one unusual case in 1998 involving a woman sentenced to death by the State of Texas. The woman, who admitted committing a brutal murder years earlier while in a drug-induced state of hysteria, asked the governor for a last-minute pardon. Citing a religious transformation that she experienced while in prison, the death-row inmate asked for clemency because of her renewed faith in God and subsequent change in life. Many religious groups, who typically support the use of the death penalty as a form of punishment, clamored in support of the converted woman. In the end, Texas Governor George W. Bush did not grant her a pardon, and she was the first woman executed in the State of Texas since 1863 and only the second woman executed since the 1976 Supreme Court ruling that reinstated capital punishment.

The national trend points out that among those who say religion is very important in their lives, three in four favor the death penalty, and 13% oppose it. Among those judging religion fairly important, 84% favor capital punishment, and 10% are opposed. But among those who consider religion not very important in their lives, 69% favor the death penalty, and 21% oppose it.

Situational Ethics

Eighteenth-century philosopher Immanuel Kant advocated for universal ethical practices, moral precepts that could be applied to all people at all times. The postmodern emphasis on relativism within the ethical arena has advanced situational ethics, which eschew absolute principles. Despite prevalent postmodernism in today's world, most Americans support ethical precepts that apply to everyone regardless of his or her situation. Over eight in ten adults in this country (83%) endorse absolute guidelines in determining good and evil in all situations. This figure rose four percentage points between 1988 and 1998. Women are even more inclined to favor universal moral precepts. Forty percent of them are in complete agreement with the idea of moral absolutes.

Younger adults tend to sanction situational ethics more often than older Americans. Thirteen percentage points separate the nation's youngest adults (ages 18 to 29) and the oldest adults (over age 65) on complete support for moral absolutes. Also, only 1% of Americans over age 65 completely disagrees with these absolutes, but 5% of young adults hold the same opinion.

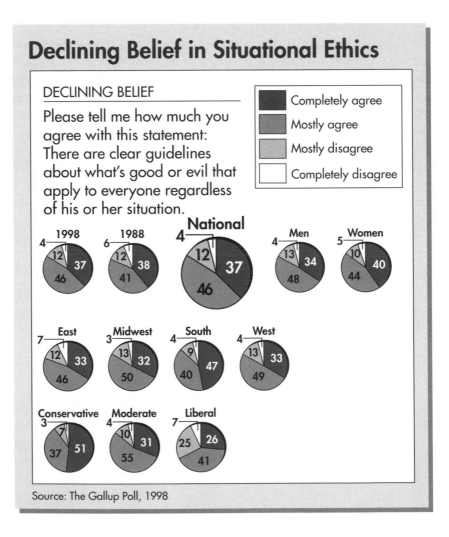

Declining Belief in Situational Ethics

DECLINING BELIEF

Please tell me how much you agree with this statement: There are clear guidelines about what's good or evil that apply to everyone regardless of his or her situation.

- ■ Completely agree
- ■ Mostly agree
- ▨ Mostly disagree
- □ Completely disagree

Source: The Gallup Poll, 1998

Southerners shun situational ethics much more than people living in other parts of the country.

Americans with postgraduate education do not hold to these unchanging standards with the same frequency as the general population. Although 37% of the nation completely agrees with these moral absolutes, 27% of adults with graduate-school education endorse the same principles. Forty-three percent of Protestants completely support these universal precepts, whereas only one Catholic in three (31%) agrees. However, personal ideology exposes the greatest differences of opinion among Americans today. Fifty-one percent of conservatives support universal ethical guidelines and only 3% of them favor situational ethics. Moderates are much less likely to express complete agreement with these moral absolutes, but they still remain supportive of moral absolutes. However, liberals in this country disagree. Nearly one in three liberals (32%)—the highest percentage of any subsection of the American population—sanctions situational ethics. Granted, relativistic values prevail much more now than they did fifty years ago, yet they are not as widespread as the ethical ambiguities that beset Americans today might suggest.

Religion and Society

Constantine ushered in the era of Christendom that dominated the Western worldview for more than fifteen hundred years. Every major nation in the Western world has a legacy of religion coupled with all spheres of society, from education to government to culture. Even the United States, born out of a struggle for religious freedom and independence, has a heritage of public expression of private religion in the realms of politics and society. H. Richard Niebuhr, building upon the work of German theologian Ernst Troeltsch, delineated five ways in which Christians have tried to resolve the tension between human culture and divine involvement. Niebuhr's category of "Christ transforming culture" epitomizes the Puritan theocracy and Protestant Americana of the first two hundred years in this country's history. During the course of the twentieth century, however, many Americans have sought to sever the ligament of religion and culture. While many religious conservatives bemoan the "de-Christianization" of America that has taken place over the past four decades, Gallup research suggests that the United States remains one of the most religiously committed nations in the world.

Americans outshine most other industrialized nations in religious fervor. While nearly all people in this country believe in God (96%), only 70% of Canadians and only 61% of Britons concur. By a much higher percentage, more Americans affirm the existence of heaven, hell, and the devil than these other English-speaking nations. Adults in the United States express twice the amount of confidence that religion's influence is increasing as compared to sentiments among adults in the United Kingdom. Three times as many Americans said they had attended church within the past week as did Britons. However, the United States does not hold a monopoly on the world's religious commitment. India has emerged as a nation of highly religious people. Nearly six in ten Indians (59%) describe themselves as very religious. Another third of the population (32%) call themselves moderately religious.

In America today the skyscrapers of industry and commerce dwarf church steeples among downtown city skylines. Yet religion still influences civic concerns to some degree. Only one quarter of the U.S. population (24%) complains that religious leaders have too much influence in the nation's politics. In fact the plurality of Americans (46%) regard clergy's political involvement to be the right amount. One area of clergy concern in the political arena involves racial harmony. The civil rights movement, which originated several decades ago with Black church leaders like Martin Luther King, Jr., has not eliminated discrimination for all Blacks in this country. Nearly one-half of Blacks (47%) report being treated unfairly in some setting within the past month. Most of them experience this while shopping, but discrimination can also occur at work, in social settings, and even while riding public transportation. Whites in the United States do not perceive discrimination as often as Blacks. Seventy-six percent of Whites perceive that Black Americans are treated the same as Whites in their local community. Only one in two Blacks (49%) agrees.

Confidence in American churches runs high. Nearly three out of five adults (59%) place their highest confidence in America's churches among all societal institutions. For the past three decades, the church or organized religion has consistently ranked at the top of the list of sixteen key American institutions. Overall confidence in society's institutions has abated over the last half century, and the church has diminished credibility and trustworthiness in the eyes of many Americans. Nonetheless, a majority of adults in this country continue to trust churches more than other institutions. The latest Gallup findings also indicate that Americans think highly of the ethics of members of the clergy in this country. Fifty-nine percent of the populace ranks the clergy's honesty and ethical standards as very high or high. Curiously, over the past nine years pharmacists have topped the list of twenty-six occupations rated for their honesty and moral standards.

Religion pervades many elements of our society. Sessions of Congress and presidential inaugurations begin with prayer. Our currency declares, "In God We Trust," and nearly all Americans affirm that motto. Granted, American pioneers like Roger Williams and Thomas Jefferson advocated a society in which a "wall of separation" existed between religion and politics. Yet the history of this nation records a tight weaving of these disparate strands. Religion galvanized many of the movements that have shaped American culture and current society including independence, abolition, suffrage, and civil rights. The economic and religious peculiarities of this country do not halt the ever-increasing engagement of Americans with international society. In light of this trend toward globalization, it will be interesting to see if and how Americans' religious faith and fervor will shape society as the United States embraces more global constituents in the twenty-first century.

The United States leads the English-speaking world in matters of faith, with levels of belief remaining consistently high in recent years, while inhabitants

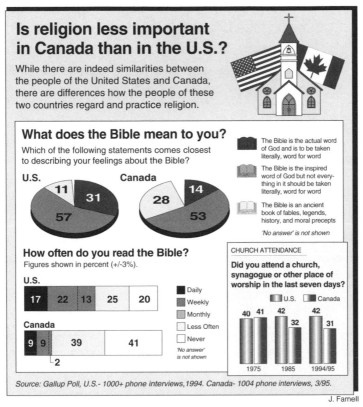

Is religion less important in Canada than in the U.S.?

While there are indeed similarities between the people of the United States and Canada, there are differences how the people of these two countries regard and practice religion.

What does the Bible mean to you?

Which of the following statements comes closest to describing your feelings about the Bible?

The Bible is the actual word of God and is to be taken literally, word for word

The Bible is the inspired word of God but not everything in it should be taken literally, word for word

The Bible is an ancient book of fables, legends, history, and moral precepts

'No answer' is not shown

U.S. — 11, 31, 57
Canada — 14, 28, 53

How often do you read the Bible?
Figures shown in percent (+/-3%).

U.S. — 17, 22, 13, 25, 20
Canada — 9, 9, 39, 41 — 2

Daily
Weekly
Monthly
Less Often
Never
'No answer' is not shown

CHURCH ATTENDANCE

Did you attend a church, synagogue or other place of worship in the last seven days?

U.S. ■ Canada ■

1975: 40, 41
1985: 42, 32
1994/95: 42, 31

Source: Gallup Poll, U.S.- 1000+ phone interviews,1994. Canada- 1004 phone interviews, 3/95.

J. Farnell

of Canada and the United Kingdom have witnessed significant declines in belief between 1980 and 1995. Nearly all adults in the United States (96%) say they believe in God or a universal spirit , but only seven in ten Canadians and six in ten Britons make similar claims. Seventy-eight percent of American adults believe there is a heaven, yet only six Canadians in ten and one-half of those in the British Isles share this belief. Similarly, belief in the devil and in hell is higher in the United States than in the United Kingdom In the United States six in ten adults believe in hell and over one-half (55%) believe in the devil. In Canada just slightly over half believe in hell whereas in the United Kingdom, only one person in four believes the same.

Levels of belief in God for Canadians have declined in the 1990s. In 1995 only 70% of Canadians claimed a belief in God; this is a rapid decline compared with figures in 1990 (86%) and 1985 (87%). The most serious declines, however, lie in Great Britain. Britons demonstrate dramatic drops in belief in many traditional articles of faith. In one instance, belief in God plunged fifteen percentage points in just fifteen years. Between 1979 and 1995, it plummeted from 76% to only 61%. Similarly, the number believing in heaven has declined from 57% to 50%. At the

America Surpasses Other Nations in Faith Matters by Belief in:

	CANADA	GREAT BRITAIN	UNITED STATES
God or universal spirit or lifeforce	70%	61%	96%
Heaven	61%	50%	78%
Hell	54%	24%	60%
The devil	57%	24%	55%
Reincarnation	33%	26%	27%

Source: The Gallup Poll, Gallup Organization, Ltd. (United Kingdom), Gallup Poll of Canada, 1995

same time belief in the devil and in hell not only remained constant but has actually increased from 22% in 1979 to 24% in 1995 for both the devil and hell.

History records that the first waves of emigrants from England came to America in search of religious freedom. Today many of their descendants still maintain a steady faith, but back home in England far fewer people take their religious beliefs as seriously as their American counterparts. Religion in the United Kingdom has been tightly woven into the fabric of British history for centuries. One cannot study British history without encountering religious luminaries such as Anselm, Thomas More, and John Wesley. Unlike the United States, Great Britain does not separate church and state. The Queen still maintains religious titles such as "Defender of the Faith," and Anglican bishops continue to comprise a portion of the House of Lords. Although church is wedded to state in Great Britain, the British people claim far less interest in religious matters than Americans. For example, among people in the United Kingdom just 17% of adults say they consider religion "very important" in their lives. By comparison, a majority of 57% of Americans take it very seriously. Additionally, born-again or evangelical Christians in the United States outnumber evangelicals in Great Britain by four to one.

British and American Faith[22]

	🇬🇧	🇺🇸
Believe Jesus Christ is...		
God or son of God	46%	84%
Just a man, another religious leader	34	9
Just a story	9	1
Other/Not sure	11	6
Membership		
Roman Catholic	14%	28%
Church of England/ Episcopalian	54	2
Church of Scotland/ Presbyterian	6	5
Other	12	58
None	14	7
Religion's Influence is...		
Increasing	12%	27%
Decreasing	73	63
Remaining about the same	10	5
Ever Pray	59%	88%
Went to church in last seven days	12%	27%

Source: The Gallup Organization Worldwide Associates, 1993

The distinctions in religious belief about Jesus Christ between the two nations is even more striking. Less than half of the people of Great Britain (46%) believe in Jesus Christ as the son of God, 34% regard him as only a historical personage, and 9% think he is just a legend. In the United States 84% of the adult population considers Jesus either God or the son of God. Just one person in ten (9%) feels he was simply another religious leader, and 1% think he is but a legend.

In the United States nine persons in ten (91%) say religion is at least somewhat important in their lives. Eight in ten Americans today (81%) consider themselves religious persons, compared to just 58% of Britons who see themselves that way. Americans are twice more likely than Britons (27% versus 12%) to regard religion's influence as increasing. Moreover, 73% of the British people today think that religion is losing its influence.

In an average week 43% of the American population visits a church or other place of worship, compared to only 14% of the people of Great Britain. Less than one Briton in four (23%) reports attending church at least monthly.

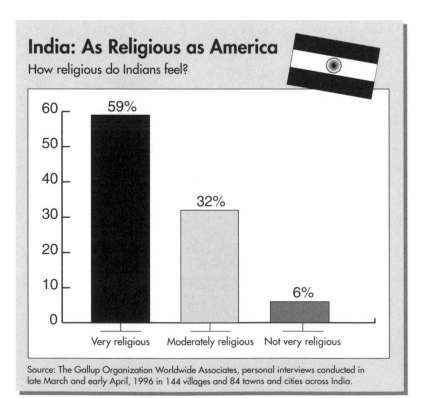

India: As Religious as America
How religious do Indians feel?

Source: The Gallup Organization Worldwide Associates, personal interviews conducted in late March and early April, 1996 in 144 villages and 84 towns and cities across India.

Social Values in India

	APPROVE	DISAPPROVE
Women who want a career outside the home	59%	21%
Women who delay getting married in order to find their education or start a career	53%	26%
People who marry someone of a lower social class	39%	38%
People who marry someone of a higher social class	34%	41%
People who marry someone of a different religion	29%	45%
Married couples who want to have as many children as possible	12%	62%
Married men who have an affair or relationship outside their marriage	12%	62%

Source: The Gallup Organization, personal interviews conducted in late March and early April, 1996 in 144 villages and 84 towns and cities across India.

RELIGION IN INDIA

An overwhelming majority of Indian adults (91%) describe themselves as religious. A minute section of the populace regard themselves as "not very religious" (6%). At the same time the stereotypes of Hindu asceticism— advocated by religious leaders like Ghandi—do not accurately reflect the ideals of contemporary Indian culture. For example, nearly half of the population (48%) chooses working hard and getting rich as the credo that best describes them. By comparison only 10% center upon a Ghandian spiritual attitude of "resisting all evils in the world and living a pure and just life." Furthermore, only 4% would embrace the extreme position of "never think of yourself; give everything in service to society."

The Western world has long criticized Indian culture as being guilty of sexism and class prejudice. Gallup research reveals some evidence of progressive thought coupled with an adherence to ancient biases. A majority of both genders approve of women who seek a career outside the home or who postpone marriage to attain educational or career goals. The caste system, however, continues to exert strong influence over Indians' opinions on social and religious issues. They continue to disapprove of someone marrying beneath his or her class; likewise, only one in three Indians approves of marrying a person of a higher social class. Many Indians still frown upon marrying someone of a different religion. There is also strong disapproval of married couples wanting to have as many children as possible given the debilitating challenges of overpopulation on the Indian Subcontinent. Finally, Indians reject the "double standard" of sexual conduct among men. Sixty-two percent of the Indian people disapprove of married men having an affair or relationship outside their marriage.

GLOBAL FAMILY VALUES

According to an international Gallup survey, the world is a long way from sharing a global set of family values. Unmarried couples desiring to have children would find the greatest support in Europe; Asian nations would be least likely to grant them approval. Americans are almost evenly divided on the issue. The survey reveals wide variation in perceptions on the ideal number of children for a family, on people's preferences for the baby's gender, and in the degree to which people consider having children to be an important part of their lives.

The issue generating the most diverse reactions, however, is the morality of unwed couples having children. In this country the debate came quickly to the fore during the early part of the 1990s. Vice President Dan Quayle attracted much attention when he criticized the popular TV sitcom *Murphy Brown* for glorifying the prospect of single motherhood. Gallup's most recent research suggests that the United States stands out as morally conflicted over the issue, with 47% of Americans saying it is wrong for a couple to have a baby if they are not married and 50% saying it is not wrong. Older Americans are the most likely to suggest that it is morally wrong (68%).

In India, Singapore, and Taiwan, a majority of adults condemn the prac-

No Global Consensus on Family Values

Do you think it is wrong for unmarried couples to bear children out of wedlock, or not?

	YES	NO
India	84%	14%
Singapore	69%	11%
Taiwan	55%	26%
United States	47%	50%
Guatemala	38%	56%
Thailand	37%	57%
Mexico	31%	67%
Canada	25%	72%
Great Britain	25%	73%
Spain	21%	73%
Lithuania	16%	75%
Hungary	16%	81%
Colombia	10%	87%
Germany	9%	90%
France	8%	91%
Iceland	3%	95%

Source: The World Gallup Survey, The Gallup Organization Worldwide Associates conducted in sixteen countries, 1997

tice of children being born out of wedlock. All other countries in this survey believed that it is not wrong, although the percentages in countries like the United States are so close that it is difficult to declare a clear majority. (This Gallup survey has an associated sampling error of plus or minus three percentage points.) In several European nations, the overwhelming majority of people support unmarried couples having children. In both Germany and France, nine out of ten adults approve of couples bearing children outside the bonds of marriage. However, Iceland provides the greatest amount of approval—with an astonishing 95% approval rating.

HOMOSEXUAL MARRIAGES

Most still disapprove of homosexual marriage

Liberal clergy are arguing for acceptance of homosexual lifestyles, same-sex marriages and ordination of homosexual clergy, while the majority of the rank-and-file members and clergy oppose these

ATTITUDE TREND

Do you feel that homosexuality should be considered an acceptable alternative lifestyle?

1996 — Yes 44 / No 50

1992 — Yes 38 / No 57

1982 — Yes 34 / No 51

'No opinion' is not shown.

ATTITUDE TREND

Do you think marriages between homosexuals should be recognized by the law as valid, with the same rights as traditional marriages?
In percent.

Should 27 — Should not 68 — No Opinion 5

Source: The Gallup Poll, 1,008 interviews conducted 3/96.   Figures (+/- 3%).

J. Farnell

Churches have struggled with the volatile issue of homosexuality as some liberal members of the clergy and laity argue for acceptance of homosexual lifestyles, same-sex marriages, and ordination of homosexual clergy, while the majority of the rank-and-file members and clergy oppose these ideas. Acceptance of homosexual lifestyles, as measured by The Gallup Poll, has grown in the United States. Nearly half of the adult population now accepts homosexuality as a lifestyle, compared to just one in three in 1982. This growing acceptance of the individual lifestyle, however, does not appear to extend to allowing homosexuals to institutionalize their sexual preferences. Far fewer people, for example, think homosexual marriages should be recognized.

In recent years certain states have attempted to sanction same-sex marriages. The States of Hawaii and Alaska are two mavericks of the Union that have made such ventures. However, during the November 1998 elections, voters in both of those states resoundingly rejected the proposed legislation.

On these issues, young women are about the only group of the populace that gives majority support to gay rights. Men, young and old, are the principal opponents. Only 34% of conservative Americans approve of legal homosexual relations—a strong contrast with the 62% of adults who claim a liberal ideology that approve of such relations. Americans who regard themselves as born again are much less likely to condone same-sex marriages. Thirty percent of born-again Americans sanction same-sex marriages while 62% of them disapprove. Distinctions can also be clearly seen among adults with varying understandings of the origin of homosexuality. Among Americans who believe that homosexuality is a predisposition that an individual is born with, 62% support legal homosexual marriages. That figure drops by half (30%) for those adults who believe homosexuality is caused by individual choice and upbringing.

CHURCH AND STATE

According to recent Gallup research, nearly eight in ten Americans (79%) support the principle of separation of church and state. Public opinion is mixed, however, on the amount of influence religious leaders can exercise on public opinion. Most Americans (46%) think that members of the clergy exert the "right amount" of influence on public opinion. The remainder of the population is almost evenly divided between a belief that religious leaders exercise "too much" influence (24%) and "too little" influence (26%) on matters of public opinion. Political conservatives are most inclined to say that religious leaders are having too little influence on public opinion; liberals more often think they already have too much.

Similarly, those who say that religion is "very important" in their own lives want members of the clergy to have greater influence across the land. Among those who say religion is only fairly important or of little importance, many would welcome a diminution of the political power of the clergy. Protestants—especially Baptists, Southern Baptists, Lutherans, and evangelicals—are more likely than the U.S. public to support strong religious influence on the law.

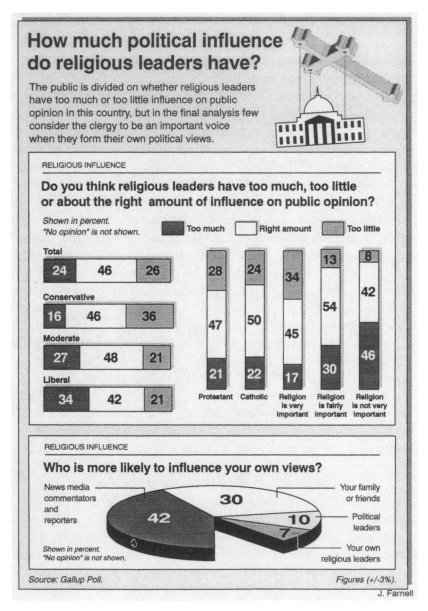

How much political influence do religious leaders have?

The public is divided on whether religious leaders have too much or too little influence on public opinion in this country, but in the final analysis few consider the clergy to be an important voice when they form their own political views.

RELIGIOUS INFLUENCE

Do you think religious leaders have too much, too little or about the right amount of influence on public opinion?

Shown in percent.
"No opinion" is not shown.

Too much | Right amount | Too little

	Too much	Right amount	Too little
Total	24	46	26
Conservative	16	46	36
Moderate	27	48	21
Liberal	34	42	21

	Protestant	Catholic	Religion is very important	Religion is fairly important	Religion is not very important
Too little	28	24	34	13	8
Right amount	47	50	45	54	42
Too much	21	22	17	30	46

RELIGIOUS INFLUENCE

Who is more likely to influence your own views?

News media commentators and reporters — 42
30 — Your family or friends
10 — Political leaders
7 — Your own religious leaders

Shown in percent.
"No opinion" is not shown.

Source: Gallup Poll. Figures (+/-3%).

J. Farnell

Opinion against such influence appears stronger among non-evangelicals than Americans nationwide.

In related Gallup studies, few Americans profess that the clergy have, in fact, influenced their own views. Although ministers obviously influence parishioners on certain personal and moral decisions, less than one person in ten (7%) says that religious leaders are most likely to influence their own views on current political issues. Far more Americans look to the media (42%) or to their family and friends (30%) for guidance in public affairs.

RACE RELATIONS

Whites and Blacks disagree greatly in their perceptions of how well Blacks are faring in our society and how they are treated in the local community. These gaps are, in some instances, smaller than they were in the 1960s, but they have not narrowed in recent years. On average, Blacks are much more likely to perceive discrimination and unfair treatment in the local community than are Whites. Three in four Whites (76%) believe that Blacks are treated the same as Whites, but only one in two Blacks (49%) hold the same sentiment. This is, however, an increase from perceptions among the Black community thirty years ago. At that time, only one in four Blacks (26%) believed that they were treated the same as Whites in their community. In 1997 there was a twenty-seven-point gap between Whites and Blacks in terms of "sameness" treatment in the local community; almost the exact same degree of divergence appeared in the 1990 Gallup survey.

Opinions among White Americans have not changed significantly within the past thirty years. In 1968 73% of them believed that Blacks in their community received the same treatment that Whites received; in 1997, that same statistic had changed only three points to 76%. Therefore, the narrowing of the gap between opinions of Blacks and Whites has developed due to changes in perceptions held by Black Americans. Gallup research reveals that 1987 was the year in which the least amount of divergence could be seen between opinions among Blacks and Whites. That year, only twenty percentage points separated the two groups. The gap has widened since then, but not nearly to the degree that existed in the 1960s and early 1970s.

Nearly one in two Black Americans (47%) cite some form of discrimination that they have encountered within the past thirty days. Among five different arenas in which discrimination has typically existed in previous years, shopping in a store is the singular place in which a plurality of Blacks have experienced discrimination. One in three Blacks (30%) say that they have been unfairly treated while shopping in a store recently. One in five Blacks

(21%) felt unfairly treated in their workplaces or in social settings such as restaurants, bars, or theaters. Contrary to a few widely publicized incidents of racial discrimination that involved law enforcement officers in recent years, only 15% of Blacks say that they have been unfairly treated in their dealings with the police.

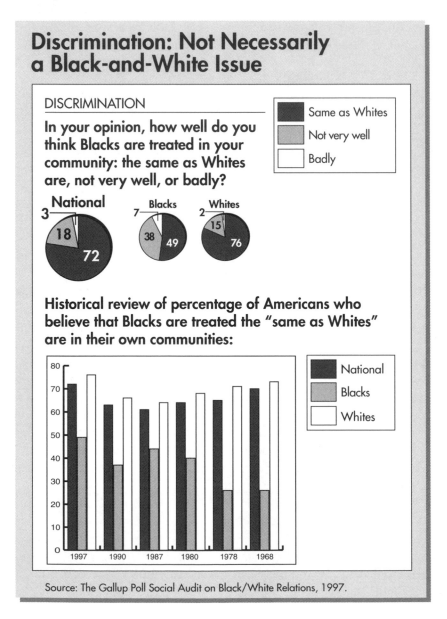

Discrimination: Not Necessarily a Black-and-White Issue

DISCRIMINATION

In your opinion, how well do you think Blacks are treated in your community: the same as Whites are, not very well, or badly?

- ■ Same as Whites
- ▨ Not very well
- □ Badly

National
3
18
72

Blacks
7
38 49

Whites
2
15
76

Historical review of percentage of Americans who believe that Blacks are treated the "same as Whites" are in their own communities:

- ■ National
- ▨ Blacks
- □ Whites

(Bar chart, years: 1997, 1990, 1987, 1980, 1978, 1968; y-axis 0 to 80)

Source: The Gallup Poll Social Audit on Black/White Relations, 1997.

Within the Black community, younger males experience the greatest degree of discrimination. Although only 30% of Blacks on average are unfairly treated while shopping in a store, 45% of Black males who are ages 18 to 34 say they experienced discrimination while shopping. Furthermore, young Black males are twice as likely as the average Black American to be treated unjustly when dealing with police (34% compared to 15%). Seventy percent of young Black males perceive discrimination in at least one of these settings, compared to the 47% average among all Blacks interviewed in the Gallup survey.

Income level does not eliminate perceived discrimination. In some situations such as shopping and dining out, wealthier Blacks are more likely to report discrimination than are those with lower incomes. Contact with police, however, is the one area where lower-income Blacks do report more discrimination. Blacks who live in the South do not report any greater degree of discrimination than those in other parts of the country. To the contrary, in some instances—such as shopping and dining out—Blacks in the South report

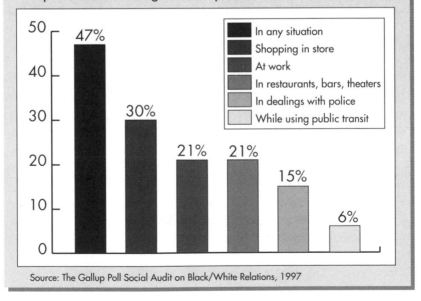

One-Half of Blacks Experience Discrimination
(Asked of only Black respondents): Can you think of any occasion in the last thirty days when you felt you were treated unfairly in the following places because you were Black? How about in a store where you were shopping? At a place of work? In a restaurant, bar, theater, or other entertainment place? While using public transportation? In dealings with the police, such as traffic incidents?

Legend:
- In any situation
- Shopping in store
- At work
- In restaurants, bars, theaters
- In dealings with police
- While using public transit

47% — In any situation
30% — Shopping in store
21% — At work
21% — In restaurants, bars, theaters
15% — In dealings with police
6% — While using public transit

Source: The Gallup Poll Social Audit on Black/White Relations, 1997

Incidence of Unfair Treatment in Selected Situations within the Last 30 Days

(Asked of only Black respondents): Can you think of any occasion in the last thirty days when you felt you were treated unfairly in the following places because you were Black? How about in a store where you were shopping? At a place of work? In a restaurant, bar, theater, or other entertainment place? While using public transportation? In dealings with the police, such as traffic incidents?

	SHOPPING IN STORE	AT WORK	RESTAURANTS BARS THEATERS	DEALINGS WITH POLICE	PUBLIC TRANSIT
U.S. Blacks	30%	21%	21%	15%	6%
Black males, ages 18–34	45%	23%	32%	34%	12%
Black males, ages 35 and over	25%	26%	19%	17%	8%
Black females, ages 18–34	28%	13%	24%	8%	2%
Black females, ages 35 and over	26%	23%	15%	9%	3%

Source: The Gallup Poll Social Audit on Black/White Relations, 1997

lower levels of perceived discrimination.

CARE FOR THE POOR

Like it or not, religious organizations in this country will likely have to shoulder more responsibility in caring for the poor and needy. Many national leaders, including Newt Gingrich, have pressed within recent years for the elimination of many government-sponsored welfare benefits. In its place, they urge organizations from the private sectors—primarily religious bodies—to take up the task of caring for the nation's poor. The people of this country, however, reject that notion by a two-to-one margin. Fifty-five percent of adults think that the government should be more responsible for assisting the poor and disenfranchised members of society, but only 28% of adults think the burden should be *primarily* carried by religious organizations.

Opinion on the issue divides largely according to political ideology.

Democrats are much more likely than Republicans to place the major responsibility in the hands of government (70% compared with 43%). Similarly, 74% of Americans who claim a liberal ideology support the gov-

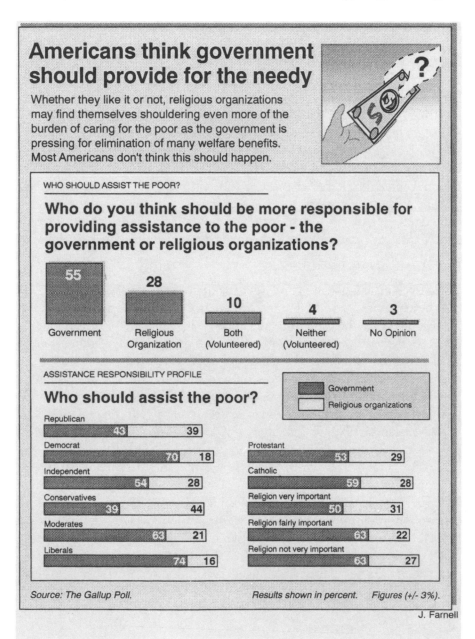

Americans think government should provide for the needy

Whether they like it or not, religious organizations may find themselves shouldering even more of the burden of caring for the poor as the government is pressing for elimination of many welfare benefits. Most Americans don't think this should happen.

WHO SHOULD ASSIST THE POOR?

Who do you think should be more responsible for providing assistance to the poor - the government or religious organizations?

55	28	10	4	3
Government	Religious Organization	Both (Volunteered)	Neither (Volunteered)	No Opinion

ASSISTANCE RESPONSIBILITY PROFILE

Who should assist the poor?

■ Government
□ Religious organizations

Republican
43 | 39

Democrat
70 | 18

Independent
54 | 28

Conservatives
39 | 44

Moderates
63 | 21

Liberals
74 | 16

Protestant
53 | 29

Catholic
59 | 28

Religion very important
50 | 31

Religion fairly important
63 | 22

Religion not very important
63 | 27

Source: The Gallup Poll.   Results shown in percent.   Figures (+/- 3%).

J. Farnell

ernment as the primary source of welfare assistance.

Despite the numerous biblical injunctions for the believing community to provide for the poor and hungry, those who say religion is "very important" in their lives do not stray very far from opinions held at the national level. Furthermore, the percentage of those who say religion is "fairly" or "not very important" and who support government-directed welfare is even higher than the statistics on the national level.

In a related Gallup survey, nearly one American in six believes he could become homeless. Eighty-six percent of the populace feels sympathy for the homeless; nearly one in three also says his sympathy is now greater than it was five years ago. Among those reporting an increase in sympathy, the majority said this change was based, at least in part, on recognition that they themselves could someday become homeless. On the matter of care for the homeless, national opinions differ from the broader topic of church- or state-supported welfare. Whereas the majority of Americans believe that the government should be the primary provider of welfare, two persons in three think that private charities are currently the best equipped to rehabilitate the homeless.

CONFIDENCE IN U.S. INSTITUTIONS

Based upon the latest Gallup findings on confidence in American institutions, the church exerts a powerful influence on current society. Out of sixteen key institutions listed, the church and the military score highest on the confidence scale. For the past twenty-five years, the church or organized religion has consistently ranked at the top of the list with nearly six in ten Americans (59%) expressing a "great deal" or "quite a lot" of confidence in the institution. As a trend, the church, the military, and the Supreme Court vie each year for the position of most trusted institution in American society; the three trade places in the ranking usually based upon the latest scandals and conflicts that ensnare each of the institutions.

In the latter portion of the 1990s, the church has been reinstated to its position as most-trusted institution—a position that it held from 1973 until 1985. In 1985, the U.S. military succeeded in garnering the most public confidence. The nation's Supreme Court reigns as the most consistently trusted branch of government. However, people in this country place confidence in other segments of the federal government including the presidency. Americans ascribe the least amount of trust to the criminal justice system, organized labor, and big business.

Confidence in U.S. institutions has eroded since the 1960s. None of the

Americans Place Highest Confidence in Churches

Please tell me how much confidence you yourself have in each one of the following—a great deal, quite a lot, some, or very little? [23]

	GREAT DEAL	QUITE A LOT	SOME	VERY LITTLE	NONE/NO OPINION
Organized religion, church	34%	25%	26%	12%	3%
Military	33%	31%	25%	8%	3%
U.S. Supreme Court	24%	26%	34%	12%	4%
Banks	16%	24%	43%	14%	3%
Public schools	16%	21%	40%	20%	3%
Newspapers	14%	19%	44%	20%	3%
Congress	10%	18%	48%	20%	4%
Television news	15%	19%	40%	24%	2%
Organized labor	11%	15%	45%	22%	7%
The presidency	25%	28%	29%	15%	3%
Police	26%	32%	30%	10%	2%
Medical system	16%	24%	40%	18%	2%
Criminal justice system	9%	15%	40%	32%	4%
Big business	11%	19%	43%	23%	4%
Small business	25%	31%	34%	9%	1%
Business and industry	18%	33%	38%	7%	4%

Source: The Gallup Poll, 1998

Trend of Confidence in the Church[24]

1998	59%
1997	56%
1996	57%
1995	57%
1994	54%
1993	53%
1991 (October)	56%
1991 (March)	59%
1990	56%
1989	52%
1988	59%
1987	61%
1986	57%
1985	66%
1984	64%
1983	62%
1981	64%
1979	65%
1977	64%
1975	68%
1973	66%

Source: The Gallup Poll, 1998

sixteen institutions in this study receive as high marks in 1998 as they did twenty or thirty years ago. For example, in the early 1970s, an average public confidence score for the church or organized religion was sixty-seven points (out of a possible one hundred). In the late 1970s and early 1980s, that average score fell to sixty-four points. Between 1988 and 1998, the average marker has dropped even further to fifty-nine points. All U.S. institutions find themselves in the same situation: fewer Americans today express a "great deal" or "quite a lot" of confidence in the various institutions of society than they did ten, fifteen, and twenty-five years ago.

ETHICS OF OCCUPATIONS

For the ninth consecutive year, America's pharmacists top Gallup's list of twenty-six occupations rated for their honesty and ethical standards. Pharmacists are recognized by 69% of Americans—an all-time high for any profession measured in the Gallup study—for having "high" or "very high" standards. Four other groups receive plaudits from a majority of Americans in Gallup's 1997 annual survey: the clergy, medical doctors, college teachers, and dentists.

About one person in six (17%) gives the clergy a "very high" rating on honesty and ethics, while 42% rate their performance "high." Thirty-one percent say "average," and six percent grade the clergy with a score of "low" or "very low" on this integrity scale. The current figures for clergy represent an upward four-year trend since 1993; clergy scored six points higher in 1997 than they did in 1993. Clergy integrity scores in 1993 were the lowest they have ever been for the Gallup study with a score of fifty-three points. In 1985, the clergy obtained the highest score on Gallup's survey of occupational honesty and integrity; that year, two out of three Americans (67%) rated the honesty and ethical standards of clergy members as "high" or "very high."

Many professions, including journalists, business executives, building contractors, and real estate agents are considered just "average" on Gallup's integrity scale. A few occupations, particularly car salespeople and lawyers, stand out for having relatively pronounced negativity ratings. Collectively, the occupations that adults brand with the lowest scores for honesty and ethics on a consistent basis are those that involve public service and selling. Only about one person in ten rates the ethics of senators, advertising practitioners, members of Congress, insurance salespeople, and car salespeople in positive terms. Indeed, about four in ten rate each of these occupations as very low or low. Car sales associates have held the dubious honor of finishing dead last every

Pharmacists, Clergy Are Most Highly Rated Occupations

Please tell me how you would rate the honesty and ethical standards of people in these different fields—very high, high, average, low or very low?

	PERCENTAGE SAYING VERY HIGH OR HIGH		PERCENTAGE SAYING VERY HIGH OR HIGH
Druggists/ Pharmacists	69%	Local officeholders	20%
Clergy	59%	Building contractors	20%
Medical doctors	56%	Newspaper reporters	19%
College teachers	55%	Stockbrokers	18%
Dentists	54%	State officeholders	17%
Police	49%	Real estate agents	16%
Engineers	49%	Lawyers	15%
Funeral directors	36%	Labor union leaders	15%
Bankers	34%	Senators	14%
Public opinion pollsters	23%	Advertising practitioners	12%
Journalists	23%	Congress members	12%
TV reporters/ Commentators	22%	Insurance salespeople	12%
Business executives	20%	Car salespeople	8%

Source: The Gallup Organization, 1997

Clergy Ratings

Below is the trend for clergy integrity ratings:

	PERCENTAGE RATING CLERGY VERY HIGH OR HIGH
1997	59%
1996	56%
1995	56%
1994	54%
1993	53%
1992	54%
1991	57%
1990	55%
1988	60%
1985	67%
1983	64%
1981	63%
1977	61%

Source: The Gallup Poll, 1997

year since their initial appearance on the Gallup survey in 1977.

SOCIAL CONCERNS

Americans are taking a hard line on many social issues, especially those pertaining to matters of life and death. Currently, eight in ten say they favor the death penalty for murder and life sentences for drug dealers. Two adults in

Citizens Vote on Social Issues

Suppose that you could vote on key issues as well as candidates on election day. Please tell me whether you would vote for or against each of the following propositions.

	FOR	AGAINST
Life sentences for drug dealers	80%	17%
Death penalty for murder	79%	18%
Prayer in public schools amendment	73%	25%
2-year cutoff for welfare recipients without work	71%	24%
Doctor-assisted suicide	68%	29%
Teaching creationism in public schools	58%	36%
Ban on partial-birth abortions	57%	39%
5-year ban on immigration	50%	46%
Reduce social spending	44%	53%
Abortion ban except to save the mother's life	42%	56%
School busing for racial balance	34%	62%
Racial preferences in jobs/schools	14%	83%

Source: The Gallup Poll, 1996

three endorse physician-assisted suicide to end a patient's life by some painless means if the patient and his or her family request it.

Abortion continues to be a volatile topic that transcends society's categorical boundaries of politics, gender, and religion. A majority of the public supports a ban on late-term procedures known as "partial-birth" abortions. This does not necessarily indicate the public's support of a return to abortion practices prior to 1973. For example, many Americans oppose more sweeping bans that would disallow all abortions except those intended to save the mother's life. In spiritual matters, widespread support continues for a constitutional amendment to allow prayer in the public schools, with nearly three persons in four saying they would vote for such a change. A majority would favor the teaching of "creationism" as well as evolution in the schools, even though the courts have consistently disallowed it because it is considered spiritual rather than a scientific theory, and it thereby violates the separation between church and state.

Welfare programs remain unpopular, with seven persons in ten supporting a two-year cutoff in cases in which the recipient has failed to find work in the period. A slim majority of Americans (53%), however, oppose sweeping overall cuts in social spending for health, education, and welfare. Advanced civil rights causes find fewer supporters nowadays. Just one person in three favors continued school busing to achieve racial balance. Only 14% approve of affirmative action policies to achieve racial balances in jobs and schooling. One of the most surprising responses from Gallup research relates to immigration. Half the nation would vote for a five-year ban on legal immigration.

Religion and Youth

The teenager is an American invention, both envied and feared throughout the world. Whether the rest of the world likes it or not, sooner or later the music they hear will be influenced by American young people's musical tastes, and so will the movies and the television they see. Increasingly the diet of the world features "junk food" originally designed to appeal to American teen tastes, and youth around the globe covet American jeans and leather jackets that ultimately become incorporated into the designs of the fashion houses of Paris, Milan, and Tokyo. Certainly teen fads change with shocking rapidity, and discerning consistency among American teen religious beliefs could prove impossible. However, certain trends in young people's beliefs transcend seasonal whims.

The Gallup Youth Survey has recorded teen beliefs for nearly three decades. Through the years, many religious adults feared that teens might join cults, flirt with Satanism, or reject the religious mores of American culture; however, during the final decades of the twentieth century, most young people have mirrored the religious preferences and practices of their parents and other adults. In many cases, youth surpass their parents in church involvement and religious practice. For example, in a typical week nearly half of the teens in this country attend religious services at least once. This is eight percentage points higher than adult attendance (42%). Over half of this nation's young people affiliate with a Protestant faith (52%). Another quarter of the teen population practices Roman Catholicism (26%). The remaining young people embrace the Jewish faith, Orthodoxy, Mormonism, no particular faith group, or other religious faiths.

American young people express great confidence in their eclipsing the charity and faith of their parents. Sixty-five percent of the nation's youth are "very" or "somewhat" confident that they will be more religious than their parents. An even greater percentage of them (85%) believe they will spend more time helping others than their parents currently do. Young people also demonstrate greater inclinations for tolerance. For example, college freshmen welcome people of various religious faiths as roommates. Among incoming college students, Christians are welcomed the most of any major religious group. The percentage of approval approximates the percentage of the country who claim Christian beliefs. However, American college freshmen also embrace Jews and Muslims as potential roommates with very high levels of approval. In fact, American young people prefer a roommate of any major faith group over a roommate who is atheist or agnostic.

The religious fervor has cooled slightly over the last fifty years of the twentieth century. For example, in the 1950s and 1960s, 83% of young people believed in a personal God who observes, rewards, and punishes. By the 1990s, that figure had dropped to 76%. Belief in the Bible's inerrancy tumbled an even greater extent—twenty-three percentage points between the 1960s and the 1990s. Incidentally, this reflects changes in adult opinions on biblical inerrancy. Church attendance among young people, although still better than among today's adults, is significantly lower than it was in the 1950s and 1960s, when attendance figures peaked at 70% of the teen population.

In theory, most U.S. adults favor religious influence in the lives of our nation's young people. Over 90% of Americans think that honesty, democracy, patriotism, moral courage, the Golden Rule, and caring for friends and family should be integrated into the curriculum of public schools. Moreover, nearly seven in ten people (69%) suppose that their local communities could reach consensus on a set of basic values to be taught in the local public schools. Programs in character education have emerged in numerous public school districts at the end of this century with the intention of raising up a kinder, more ethical generation of students.

Two out of three adults also favor prayer in the public schools. Prayer in public schools, which in several places continued long after the Supreme Court's 1962 ruling that outlawed its practice, has maintained support since the first Gallup study on the matter in 1974. Support diminishes somewhat when the specifics of prayer in school are elaborated. Sixty-five percent of adults favor prayers from many different faiths whereas 24% of the nation prefer strictly Christian prayers. The debate intensifies on the matter of who chooses the prayer—parents, students, teachers, administrators, or the school board.

An overwhelming majority of people in the United States endorse religion in public school education. Nearly eight in ten adults do not object to comparative religious studies as part of the curriculum. Three out of four sanction elective courses in biblical studies as well as using the Bible in literature, history, and social studies classes. With such strong support, it is surprising to discover that the percentage of schools already doing these things pales in comparison.

Even more Americans approve of sex education in public schools. Eighty-seven percent of adults support sex education as part of the high school curriculum. This approval rating has climbed steadily since the early 1980s. The greatest opposition arises from parents of students who attend nonpublic schools, but even this group strongly supports sex education in schools (78%). Most Americans want young people to be familiar with the biological aspects of sex such as venereal diseases, AIDS, and the biology of reproduction. Exploring moral dilemmas such as abortion and homosexuality in the classroom does not receive nearly the same degree of public favor.

Teen Church Attendance

For decades Americans have placed the dreams and hopes of the nation upon the shoulders of its young people. Our nation's young people live in an era of intense specialization and dramatic differentiation. In our culture of cornucopia options, from coffee flavors to college choices, the youth of our country will encounter even more choices and challenges in the faith dimension of their lives as they approach the next millennium.

More Teens Than Adults in Church Today

TEENS ATTENDING CHURCH

Have you attended church or synagogue in the last seven days?

Nationally	50%
Male	48%
Female	52%
Protestant	60%
Catholic	56%
White-collar background	52%
Blue-collar background	48%

How important is it for parents to go to church or other places of worship with teens?

Very important	38%
Not very important	27%
Somewhat important	35%

What is your religious preference?

Protestant	52%
Roman Catholic	26%
None	9%
Other	8%
Mormon	3%
Jewish	2%
Orthodox	Less than 1%

Percentage of teen church attendance

1995	50%
1993	49%
1987	52%
1984	51%
1982	50%
1979	49%
1977	47%

Source: The Gallup Poll, 1995

Measurements taken by The Gallup Youth Survey since 1977 demonstrate that teen church attendance at houses of worship on average has been slightly better than 50%. Moreover, teen church attendance is higher than that of adults. 1992 saw the lowest dip in youth worship attendance, but even in that year 45% of America's youth said they had attended some type of church or synagogue within the last seven days. The strongest showing of youth church attendance occurs among American Protestants; three in five of them had attended church within the last seven days. Young people often endorse the idea that parents and their children should attend church together. Only 27% of the teen population expressed reluctance to have parents and teens in worship services together. This notion runs counter to the ever-growing phenomenon of youth-only worship services that have begun at myriad churches during the latter portion of the twentieth century.

Over eight teenagers in ten in this country claim adherence to one of the Judeo-Christian faiths as their religious preference. Teens are twice as likely to prefer a Protestant faith than a Catholic one by 52% to 26%. Protestant teens are particularly concentrated in the South and Midwest. The Roman Catholic faith draws its largest following in the East, where 37% of teenagers say it is their religious faith preference. American young people are more likely to have no church preference than they are to prefer Mormonism, Judaism, Orthodoxy, or various other religious faiths. Although 9% state that they have no religious preference, only a slim number assert that they are either atheists or agnostics.

TEENS AND PARENTS

Despite the prevailing notion that teenagers in our country are more self-centered than previous generations, Gallup survey research suggests an interest among many American young people to be more religious and more charitable than their parents. Two teens in three say they are confident that they will be more religious than their parents. That figure leaps to over three in four among teens who had recently attended church. Those young people who had not recently attended church doubt that they will be more religious than their parents. Obviously, the trend suggests that church attendance influences the young person's inclination for future involvement in religious faith.

Even more teens express confidence in their charity. Most young people think that they will spend more time than their parents do now in helping other people. The desire and expectation to be a caregiver is spread among teens from all walks of life. Female teenagers express greater confidence than their male counterparts that they will spend more time helping other people than their parents have (47% of females versus 33% of males). It is also interesting to note that church attendance does not influence the teenager's interest in spending more time helping people—the figures are strikingly similar between those who had attended church recently and those who had not.

Teens plan to be more religious and giving than their parents

Are America's young losing their faith and becoming more selfish? They don't think so. Their elders will be relieved to know that many teen-agers expect to be more religious and more charitable than their parents.

■	Very	
▨	Somewhat	
□	Not too	

FUTURE RELIGIOUS FAITH

How confident are you that you will be more religious than your parents?

National

			Attended church last week	Did not attend church
35 / 22 / 43	Male 37 / 20 / 42	Female 32 / 24 / 44	23 / 29 / 48	44 / 17 / 39

All figures shown in percent.

FUTURE CHARITY

How confident are you that you will spend more time helping other people?

National

			Attended church last week	Did not attend church
15 / 39 / 46	Male 18 / 33 / 49	Female 11 / 47 / 42	13 / 44 / 43	15 / 36 / 49

Source: The Gallup Youth Survey, 7/95-10/95.   *Figures (+/- 4%).*

J. Farnell

RELIGION IN SCHOOLS

Two in three adults (69%) advocate that basic character values should be taught in U.S. public schools. The feeling is even greater among those who currently have children in the schools. Despite the challenge of reaching consensus on what these core values might be, Gallup research suggests there are several "bedrock" values that are supported by over nine in ten Americans. Nearly everyone (97%) believes that honesty should be taught. Another topic of

The good ole' golden rule days?

Parents and teens agree that values like honesty and patriotism should be taught in schools . . .

Adults ████ Teens

100%

97
96

93

91

90

90%

87

84

85

84

80%

. . . but fewer teens believe that the "golden rule" is one of them.

75

70%

| Honesty | Different Religious beliefs | Patriotism or love of country | Democracy | "The Golden Rule" * |

* "Do unto others as you would have others do unto you."

Source: George H. Gallup Jr. Teen poll based on telephone interviews with 518 teen-agers, ages 13-17 in 1993 & 1994. Could vary 4 percentage points. Adult survey based on telephone interviews with 1,306 adults in 1993. Plus or minus 3 percentage points.

J. Trigg

strong consensus is democracy. Following democracy, Americans equally favor (91%) teaching moral courage, caring for friends and family members, as well as patriotism—that is, love of one's country. Americans also favor a curriculum that reinforces the Golden Rule of doing unto others as you would have them do unto you. Support wanes slightly for schools to teach students to accept people unlike themselves. Although 87% of the nation thinks that schools should teach acceptance of diverse religious beliefs, the number drops to 73% for acceptance of people who hold unpopular or controversial political and social views. Just over one in two adults (56%) think that schools should teach students to accept the right of a woman to choose abortion. The least amount of public support for character education in public schools deals with accepting homosexuals or bisexuals. Only 51% of adults favor an education that teaches acceptance of people with different sexual orientations.

Both Protestants and Catholics follow the national averages on all of the items Gallup surveyed regarding character education in our nation's schools. The Jewish community, however, departed from the national average on a few issues. For example, Jews are less likely to favor teaching the Golden Rule than most Americans. However, on matters of accepting people unlike ourselves, Jews are much more consistently supportive than the general population. The Jewish approval rating of teaching students about accepting people of different religious beliefs is four points higher than their Protestant and Catholic partners. Jews are ten percentage points higher than the national average on the topic of teaching students to accept people who hold unconventional and unpopular views in the area of politics or society. But the most significant point of departure deals with sexual orientation. The Jewish approval rating for teaching our nation's students about accepting homosexuals or bisexuals is a staggering thirty-four percentage points higher than the national average and forty points higher than the Protestants' rating. Even though the number of Jews in the national sample is small, differences of opinion are great enough to draw broad conclusions. Moreover, these conclusions are consistent with findings in other surveys.

Americans—at both the national and individual level—have fiercely debated the issue of school prayer since the 1962 Supreme Court ruling that organized prayer in public schools is not permissible under the First Amendment. In 1963, 70% of the public disapproved of this decision, and many efforts at passing a constitutional amendment to allow school prayer have been made since then. In 1984 Ronald Reagan joined many in calling for such a constitutional amendment. Ten years later, Newt Gingrich sparked debate when soon after the Republicans captured the House and Senate he

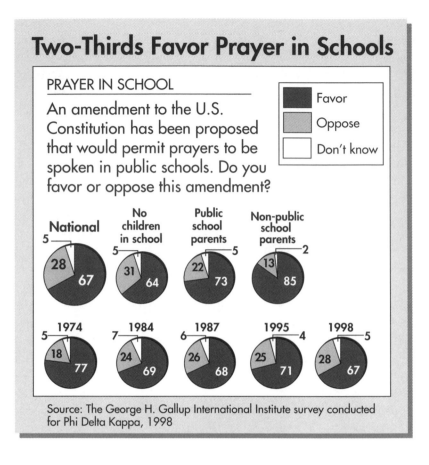

Two-Thirds Favor Prayer in Schools

PRAYER IN SCHOOL

An amendment to the U.S. Constitution has been proposed that would permit prayers to be spoken in public schools. Do you favor or oppose this amendment?

■ Favor
▨ Oppose
□ Don't know

National — 5, 28, 67
No children in school — 5, 31, 64
Public school parents — 5, 22, 73
Non-public school parents — 2, 13, 85

1974 — 5, 18, 77
1984 — 7, 24, 69
1987 — 6, 26, 68
1995 — 4, 25, 71
1998 — 5, 28, 67

Source: The George H. Gallup International Institute survey conducted for Phi Delta Kappa, 1998

announced that the amendment would be one of his top priorities in the first one hundred days of the new Congress. The new Republican leadership quickly backed away from the issue, despite the evidence that shows a majority of Americans favor this amendment. Two out of three Americans (67%) favor the amendment to allow prayers to be spoken in public schools. Both younger and older Americans approve of prayer in schools. The largest support comes from parents of school children who attend nonpublic schools; 85% of them favor this constitutional amendment. Other groups that offer particularly high support include Blacks (76%), Republicans (80%), those living in the South (81%), and rural residents (75%). Those less likely to favor the amendment, though still offering majority support, include political independents (56%), college graduates (56%), and those in the West (51%).

Will schools reopen to different school prayer practices?

President Clinton recently issued a special memorandum on religious activities in public schools. He ordered guidelines to be drawn up to eliminate any past misunderstandings that may have led to "religion-free school zones" in the public schools.

KEY RELIGIOUS ELEMENTS

In essence the memorandum outlined three broad areas:

- **School Prayer** - Public school students can pray to themselves. Teachers and principals cannot direct them to pray.
- **Teaching Religion** - Public schools may not give religious instruction, but they can teach the history of religion and offer comparative religion courses.
- **Equal Access** - Religious activities should enjoy the same access to educational facilities that student and some secular groups now have.

BELIEF TRENDS

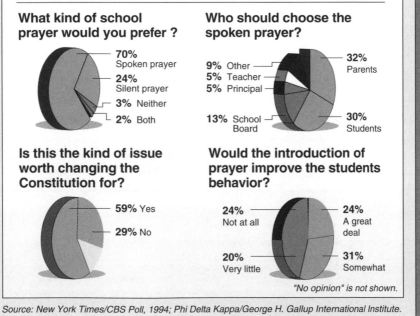

What kind of school prayer would you prefer ?

- **70%** Spoken prayer
- **24%** Silent prayer
- **3%** Neither
- **2%** Both

Who should choose the spoken prayer?

- **9%** Other
- **5%** Teacher
- **5%** Principal
- **13%** School Board
- **32%** Parents
- **30%** Students

Is this the kind of issue worth changing the Constitution for?

- **59%** Yes
- **29%** No

Would the introduction of prayer improve the students behavior?

- **24%** Not at all
- **20%** Very little
- **24%** A great deal
- **31%** Somewhat

"No opinion" is not shown.

Source: New York Times/CBS Poll, 1994; Phi Delta Kappa/George H. Gallup International Institute.

J. Farnell

Support diminishes somewhat when the specifics of prayer in school are discussed. Only 18% of adults, for instance, believe that all children should be required to participate in the public school prayer. Although the great majority of people in this country are Christians, just 24% believe public school prayers should be basically Christian. Instead, 65% of American adults favor using prayers that belong to many different religions. In 1998, about three persons in four also believe that Jewish, Muslim, and Hindu students should be allowed to say prayers from their own faith perspectives. When adults were asked in a New York Times/CBS News Poll if this matter is the kind of issue worth changing the Constitution for, 29% of Americans said no. Furthermore, little consensus can be reached on who should choose the prayer. One in three adults believe that parents should choose the prayer, another third think students should make the choice. The remaining third of the population thinks that either the school board, the principal, or the teacher should choose the prayer.[25] For that matter, most people do not even want spoken prayers, but if given a choice, believe silent prayers are more desirable (70% compared to 24%) in the public schools.

President Clinton issued a memorandum to the Attorney General and the Secretary of Education on July 12, 1995, concerning religious activities of public school students. Interpreting The Equal Access Act to allow religious

Most Americans Endorse Religion in Public Schools

Please tell me whether you would or would not object to the public schools doing the following:

... Do you happen to know whether or not the public schools of your community do the following...

	WOULD NOT OBJECT	ALREADY DOING THIS
Offering comparative religion studies	79%	29%
Offering elective courses in Bible studies	75%	8%
Using the Bible in literature, history, and social studies classes	75%	9%

Source: Gallup survey as a public service with the Laymen's National Bible Association, 1986, 1990

Views of public school students

Please tell me whether you would or would not object to the public schools... Do you happen to know whether or not the public schools of your community do the following...

	WOULD NOT OBJECT	ALREADY DOING THIS
Making facilities available after school for use by student religious groups or clubs	82%	30%
Teaching about the major religions of the world	80%	53%
Offering elective courses in Bible studies	78%	12%
Using the Bible in literature, history, and social studies classes	67%	18%

Source: Gallup Youth Survey, 1994

activity at school with the same level of access that is granted for secular activities, the Clinton administration proposed guidelines that draw approval from the great majority of Americans. President Clinton said that public schools may not provide religious instruction, but they may teach about religion (including the Bible or other Scripture), the history of religion, comparative religion, the Bible as literature, and the role of religion in the history of the United States and other nations. Both students and adults endorse these ideas, but few report that this is now taking place in our nation's schools.

Eight in ten adults and teens say they would not object to comparative religion courses. Yet, just 53% of students say this is occurring in their schools, and even fewer adults (29%) show awareness of any current course offerings of this kind. Three in four adults and students approve of offering elective courses in biblical studies in the public schools. Only about one in ten say such classes are currently offered. Three in four adults and two students in three would not object to using the Bible in literature, history, or social studies classes. Few students (18%) or adults (9%) believe this is being done now.

Among all national regions and in every major population group, heavy public support can be found for each of the religious activities named. However, a 1987 Gallup International Poll shows Americans are considerably less likely than citizens of most countries surveyed to support religion in public schools.

With the exception of comparative religion courses, to which no more than one in six in any group objects, college graduates are slightly more likely than those with less formal education to object to schools undertaking the activities surveyed. Nevertheless, support strongly outweighs opposition among college graduates as well as nongraduates.

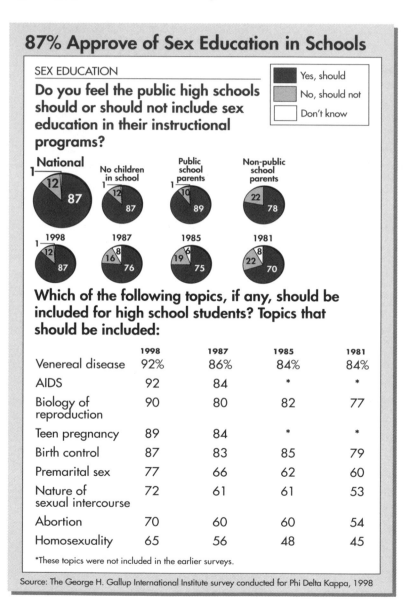

87% Approve of Sex Education in Schools

SEX EDUCATION

Do you feel the public high schools should or should not include sex education in their instructional programs?

- ■ Yes, should
- ▨ No, should not
- □ Don't know

National — 1, 12, 87

No children in school — 1, 12, 87

Public school parents — 1, 10, 89

Non-public school parents — 22, 78

1998 — 1, 12, 87

1987 — 8, 16, 76

1985 — 6, 19, 75

1981 — 8, 22, 70

Which of the following topics, if any, should be included for high school students? Topics that should be included:

	1998	1987	1985	1981
Venereal disease	92%	86%	84%	84%
AIDS	92	84	*	*
Biology of reproduction	90	80	82	77
Teen pregnancy	89	84	*	*
Birth control	87	83	85	79
Premarital sex	77	66	62	60
Nature of sexual intercourse	72	61	61	53
Abortion	70	60	60	54
Homosexuality	65	56	48	45

*These topics were not included in the earlier surveys.

Source: The George H. Gallup International Institute survey conducted for Phi Delta Kappa, 1998

By comparison, in a Gallup Poll taken in 1962, 80% of the parents of public school students said they approved of religious observances in public schools, but just 44% said such observances were taking place.

The rampant spread of AIDS and increase in teenage pregnancies has spurred an interest in including sex education in the curriculum of America's high schools. The last time Americans were queried about sex education at school, in 1987, 76% of Americans favored its inclusion. In the intervening eleven years, support has increased to 87%; this support is uniform across all population groups. Parents of students at nonpublic schools express the greatest resistance to its inclusion in high school curriculum with 22% of the group saying sex education should not be included in our schools' instructional programs. Overall support for sex education in our nation's public schools has steadily gained momentum over the past twenty years.

By a large margin, Americans want any formal sex education to include the topics of venereal disease, AIDS, the biology of the reproductive process, teen pregnancy, and birth control. One might classify these topics as the more "scientific" matters pertaining to sex education, and virtually all adults (upwards of 87%) who favor sex education in our schools want these topics to be included in the instruction. Americans are more reluctant to include some of the more "moral" issues in the curriculum for high school students. Topics such as premarital sex, abortion, and homosexuality—while still having majority approval—are not nearly as popular with American adults for inclusion in the curriculum of American schools. Nevertheless, Americans are increasingly more comfortable with including all of these topics. For instance, in 1981 only 45% of the population favored a curriculum that would discuss homosexuality. By contrast, 65% of adults in 1998 favor discussing this topic. Although not every topic has seen the dramatic increase of twenty percentage points, each item has higher percentage points than it did in 1987, 1985, and 1981.

TEEN BELIEFS

Of all supernatural and paranormal phenomena, angels rank the highest in belief among American teens. Three teens in four (76%) in the 1990s believe in angels. This represents an increase since 1978 when only 64% of American teens believed in them. Most likely to believe in angels are recent church attenders (82%), Catholic teens (81%), and young women (80%). Belief in ghosts rose in 1992 with three adolescents in ten (31%) believing in their existence; this is also an increase from 1978 when only two in ten young people affirmed belief in ghosts. More teens today also believe in astrology. Back in 1978 four in ten claimed belief in the influence of the movement of the stars and planets,

Teens Believe in the Supernatural, Not the Paranormal

Which of the following do you believe in?

	1978	1984	1986	1988	1992
Angels	64%	69%	67%	74%	76%
Astrology	40%	55%	52%	58%	54%
ESP	67%	59%	46%	50%	43%
Witchcraft	25%	22%	19%	29%	19%
Bigfoot	40%	24%	16%	22%	12%
Ghosts	20%	20%	15%	22%	31%
Clairvoyance	25%	28%	19%	21%	21%
Loch Ness Monster	31%	18%	13%	16%	11%

Source: Gallup survey conducted for the Religious Education Association of the United States and Canada, 1985

but today the figure is over one-half of teens (54%). Seventy-one percent of Hispanic teens, moreover, show interest in their horoscopes.

Belief in extrasensory perceptions (ESP), the belief that one can communicate or perceive events without the use of normal physical senses, has declined to 43% of the teen population. In 1978, two teens in three (67%) thought ESP was possible. The level of teen belief in clairvoyance—the ability to see into the future or beyond normal sensory range—has held steady. Currently, one teen in five (21%) believes in clairvoyance, which is close to the trend for the previous twenty years.

Just as belief in angels, ghosts, and astrology has increased within recent years, belief in larger-than-life creatures such as Bigfoot and Nessie, the Loch Ness monster, has steadily decreased among teens in this country. Today, only 12% of teens believe in Bigfoot. This represents the lowest level of belief in twenty years, for in 1978 four in ten American teens thought Bigfoot existed. Today, even fewer teens (11%) believe in the prehistoric creature that lives in the depths of Loch Ness in Scotland.

The opinions of teenagers in this country mirror their adult counterparts on religious issues. Almost all teens and adults (95% of each) maintain trust in God or a universal spirit. The number of teenagers who have experienced the divine presence approximates the number of adults who have encountered the same (29% of teens, 43% of adults). Adults appear to practice their faith with more frequency than teens in this country. The number of adults, for example, who pray alone frequently is almost twice the number of teens. Whereas 36% of teens read the Bible at least weekly, almost half of the adult

Young People Mirror Adult Religious Beliefs

	PERCENTAGES AMONG TEENS
Believe in God or universal spirit	95%
Believe God loves them	93%
Believe Jesus Christ is God or Son of God	86%
Personally experienced the presence of God	29%
Believe in life after death	67%
Pray alone frequently	42%
Read Bible at least weekly	36%
Have confidence in organized religion	52%
Believe religion is increasing its influence on American life	40%
Consider own religious beliefs very important	39%
Consider religion more important than parents do	27%
Believe religion can answer today's problems	25%

Source: George H. Gallup International Institute, 1993

Trends in Teen Religious Behavior and Belief

	1959–1961	1988–1993
Believe in God	97%	95%
Believe in a personal God who observes, rewards, and punishes	83%	76%
Believe in life after death	79%	67%
Believe the Bible is completely true/ literally true	62%	39%
Attended church or synagogue last week	70%	50%

Source: George H. Gallup International Institute, 1993

population (47%) reads with the same frequency. Adults also have greater confidence in organized religion (59% of adults versus 52% of teens). However, nearly three in ten teenagers (27%) say they regard religion as more important than their parents do. Based upon church attendance figures, it is clear that far more parents send their children to church than attend themselves. One in two teens said they attended church or synagogue within the last week.

Like their adult counterparts, fewer teenagers today advance strong religious convictions. Since the early 1960s, the percentage of teens who affirm life after death has dropped twelve points. The percentage of teens asserting that the Bible is completely/literally true has fallen even more significantly: twenty-three points in three decades (1959–1961 compared with 1988–1993). While 50% of American youth still attend church on a weekly basis, this represents a drop of another twenty percentage points from surveys conducted thirty years ago in 1959–1961; adult attendance has not declined to this same extent.

A remnant of teens offer optimistic positions on religion in America. Two in five teenagers view religion as increasing its influence on American life. Despite the increasing secularization of American youth, 39% of them regard their own religious beliefs as "very important." Religious belief is more important among young women than young men and among above-average students, though age has little effect on patterns of response. Southern youth are

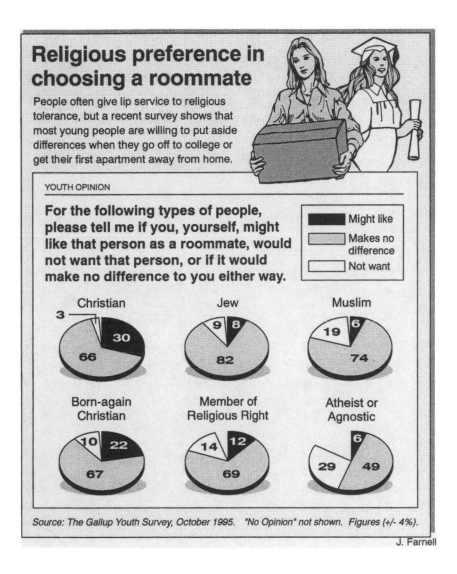

Religious preference in choosing a roommate

People often give lip service to religious tolerance, but a recent survey shows that most young people are willing to put aside differences when they go off to college or get their first apartment away from home.

YOUTH OPINION

For the following types of people, please tell me if you, yourself, might like that person as a roommate, would not want that person, or if it would make no difference to you either way.

- ■ Might like
- ▨ Makes no difference
- □ Not want

Christian
3
30
66

Jew
9 8
82

Muslim
19 6
74

Born-again Christian
10 22
67

Member of Religious Right
14 12
69

Atheist or Agnostic
6
29 49

Source: The Gallup Youth Survey, October 1995. "No Opinion" not shown. Figures (+/- 4%).

J. Farnell

far more likely to stress the importance of faith than young people in other parts of the country; however, high proportions in the East and Midwest also deem it fairly significant.

People often give lip service to religious tolerance, but survey results from a recent Gallup Youth Survey show that most young people are willing to put aside differences when they go off to college or get their first apartment away

American Teens Claim to be Religious People

RELIGIOUS TEENS

Please tell me whether you strongly agree, agree, disagree, or strongly disagree with the following statement:

You are a religious person.

	Yes, I am a religious person
National	69%
Men	69%
Women	69%
12–13 years	77%
14–15 years	63%
16–17 years	68%
White	68%
Black	75%
Hispanic	57%
Above-average students	73%
Average and below	65%
East	63%
Midwest	71%
South	77%
West	61%
Protestant	76%
Roman Catholic	72%
Church Attender	86%
Nonattender	55%

Source: Gallup Youth Survey, 1992.

from home. Their decisions offer insight to the religious prejudices they may have. Although few teens seem to show much prejudice against conventional religious beliefs, some are concerned with avoiding religious extremists and nonbelievers.

Not surprisingly in a country that is predominantly Christian, young people of that faith most often are sought as potential roommates (30%), while few teens would reject them on that basis (3%). Born-again Christians, however, are somewhat less popular, with 22% of teens saying they might enjoy having one as a roommate, while 10% would not. Teens are even more inclined to avoid members of the Religious Right (14%) than to seek them out to share an apartment or college dorm room (12%).

Faith groups outside Christianity, such as Jews or Muslims, are less likely to be sought as roommates and more often are apt to find themselves rejected. Although 82% of teens say that it would make no difference to them if a roommate were Jewish, and 8% specifically say that they would like to share accommodations with a Jew, 9% say they would avoid them. Teens also express reluctance to welcome Muslims as roommates; only 6% of America's youth would seek out a Muslim roommate.

The lack of religious belief is a far greater impediment to acceptance by teen peers than any particular professed belief. About half of the teens interviewed say it would make no difference to them if someone is an atheist or an agnostic, but just 6% would seek such a person out. In addition, nearly three in ten teens (29%) would reject them as roommates. Recent church attenders and Republican youth are the teens most likely to avoid atheists and agnostics.

A surprisingly high proportion of teens say that religion is important in their lives. Nearly seven in ten (69%) identify themselves as a "religious person"; almost one in five (19%) young people in this country strongly agree with the self-description of "a religious person." Only a scant 5% strongly disagree that they could be categorized as being religious. This is roughly equivalent with the same percent who in past surveys have said that they are agnostics or atheists, doubting or denying the existence of God.

Protestant teens are more likely than Catholic teens to strongly agree that they are religious persons, by a margin of 22% to 14%. As would be expected, most teens who said they attended church within the last week (86%) regard themselves as religious persons, but so do a majority of those who say they did not attend within the last week (55%). Religious fervor peaks in the South, where over three in four teens (77%) describe themselves as religious. Highest religious identification occurs among Black teens (75%) compared with Whites (68%) and Hispanics (57%). Students with above-average academic performance rate religious identification eight percentage points higher than other students. Likewise, teens who live in rural areas and small towns are more apt to assess themselves as religious when compared with their counterparts living in the suburbs or large cities.

notes

1. Bob Buford, *Halftime* (Grand Rapids: Zondervan, 1994).

2. Statistics do not include responses of "none" and "don't know." Consequently, figures will not always total to 100%.

3. Barnett, Lincoln, "God and the American People." *Ladies' Home Journal*, November, 1947.

4. Ibid.

5. Emerging Trends, June 1996.

6. Results add to more than 100% since many persons chose more than one category.

7. The following questions and responses are based on the 67% who say they believe they will exist in some form after death.

8. Emerging Trends, December 1996.

9. Robert Wuthnow, *Sharing the Journey: Support Groups and America's New Quest for Community* (New York: Free Press, 1994).

10. Paul Tillich, *The Shaking of the Foundations* (New York: Charles Scribner and Sons, 1948).

11. Survey responses for this year are based on those respondents who have a Bible in their household.

12. Totals add to more than 100% due to multiple responses.

13. Survey responses do not include those who gave no answer or refused to answer this question.

14. Gallup survey for the Religious Education Association of the United States and Canada, 1985.

15. James Denison, "The Cure for the Boring Church," sermon at Park Cities Baptist Church, September 6, 1998, Dallas, Texas.

16. *New York Times*/CBS News poll, 1985.

17. National Opinion Research Center poll, 1974.

18. George Washington, in his Farewell Address, September 17, 1796.

19. Gallup survey on extramarital sex, 1997.

20. Category of "no opinion" has been omitted. Also, the question has been altered slightly since first asked in the 1970s. For comparison purposes, "legal under most circumstances" and "legal only in a few circumstances" have

been combined into the category "legal in certain circumstances" used in the table above.

21. Results do not reflect 2% (national level) of respondents who claim "no opinion" on the topic.

22. The American comparisons are taken from Gallup surveys in recent years. Some differences in question wording exist on occasion, but they are not sufficient in our judgment to account for the frequent great disparity in the findings for this study.

23. Items listed in descending order according to combined totals of columns one and two, "great deal" and "quite a lot."

24. Figures represent combined totals for "great deal of confidence" and "quite a lot of confidence" in the church.

25. Source: *New York Times*/CBS News Poll, 1994.

Appendix: Gallup's Methodology

For ease in reading, responses such as "don't know" or "no answer" (usually less than 3%) are sometimes not mentioned in this book. It should also be noted that Gallup often rounds percentages to the nearest whole number. As a result, some responses will total 99% or 101%. This is a standard practice in the field of scientific surveying. Gallup has also followed the conventions of professional survey research organizations by choosing demographic titles that are easily discerned and easily understood.

Not all of the questions in this book are asked every year. The statistics cited in the first chapter of this book, Religion and Trends, are updated annually; these have served as a barometer of America's spiritual climate for several decades. In addition, Gallup seeks to track long-term trends with periodic updates for pertinent questions as mandated by current events. There is no set pattern for these updates, but they are asked as situations arise in contemporary culture.

The Gallup Poll gathers information primarily by telephone through interviews designed to provide representative samples of adults living in the continental United States. The standard size for national Gallup Polls conducted by telephone is one thousand interviews. More interviews are conducted in specific instances where greater survey accuracy is desired. The standard methods used to conduct telephone surveys and the sampling tolerances for interpreting results collected by telephone are detailed below.

Design of the Sample for Telephone Surveys

The samples of telephone numbers used in telephone interview surveys are based on a random digit stratified probability design. The sampling procedure involves stratifying the continental United States into four time zones and three city size strata within each time zone to yield a total of twelve unique strata.

In order to avoid possible bias if only listed telephone numbers are used, the Gallup Poll uses a random digit procedure designed to provide representation of both listed and unlisted (including not-yet-listed) numbers.

Samples are drawn within each strata only from "active blocks," where an "active block" is defined as one hundred contiguous telephone numbers containing three or more residential telephone listings. By eliminating non-working blocks of numbers from the sample, the likelihood that any sampled telephone number will be associated with a residence increases from only 20% (where numbers are sampled from all banks) to approximately 55%. Since most banks of telephone numbers are either substantially filled (i.e., assigned) or empty, this practical efficiency is purchased at a negligible cost in terms of possible coverage bias.

The sample of telephone numbers drawn by this method is designed to produce, with proper adjustments for differential sampling rates, an unbiased random sample of telephone households in the continental United States.

Telephone Survey Weighting Procedures

After the survey data have been collected and processed, each respondent is assigned a weight so that the demographic characteristics of the total weighted sample of respondents matches the latest estimates of the demographic characteristics of the adult population available from the U.S. Census Bureau. Telephone surveys are weighted to match the characteristics of the adult population living in households with access to a telephone.

The procedures described above are designed to produce samples approximating the adult civilian population (18 and older) living in private households (that is, excluding those in prisons, hospitals, hotels, religious and educational institutions, and those living on reservations or military bases), and households with access to a telephone. Survey percentages may be applied to census estimates of the size of these populations to project percentages into numbers of people. The manner in which the sample is drawn also produces a sample which approximates the distribution of private households in the United States; therefore, survey results can also be projected to numbers of households.

Telephone Survey Sampling Tolerances

In interpreting survey results, it should be borne in mind that all sample surveys are subject to sampling error; that is, the extent to which the results may differ from what would be obtained if the whole population surveyed had been interviewed. The size of such sample errors depends largely on the number of interviews. The following tables may be used in estimating the sampling error of any percentage in this report. The computed allowances have taken into account the effect of the sample design upon sampling error. They may be interpreted as indicating the range (plus or minus the figure shown) within which the results of repeated sampling in the same time period could be expected to vary, 95% of the time, assuming the same sampling procedure, the same interviewers and the same questionnaire.

Table A: Recommended Allowance for Sampling Error of a Percentage in Percentage Points
(at 95 in 100 confidence level)*

Sample Size:	1000	750	600	400	200	100
Percentages near 10	2	3	3	4	5	7
Percentages near 20	3	4	4	5	7	9
Percentages near 30	4	4	4	6	8	10
Percentages near 40	4	4	5	6	8	11
Percentages near 50	4	4	5	6	8	11
Percentages near 60	4	4	5	6	8	11
Percentages near 70	4	4	4	6	8	10
Percentages near 80	3	4	4	5	7	9
Percentages near 90	2	3	3	4	5	7

*The chances are 95 in 100 that the sampling error is not larger than the figures shown.

Table A shows how much allowance should be made for the sampling error of a percentage. The table would be used in the following manner: Let us say a reported percentage is 33 for a group that included one thousand respondents. First we go to the row "Percentages near 30" and go across to the column headed "1000." The number at this point is 3, which means that the 33% obtained in the sample is subject to a sampling error of plus or minus three points. Another way of saying it is that very probably (95 chances out of 100) the average of repeated samplings would be somewhere between 30% and 36%, with the most likely figure the 33% obtained.

In comparing survey results among different groups within the same sample, such as, for example, men and women, the question arises as to how large the difference between them must be before one can be reasonably sure that it reflects a real difference. In the following tables, the number of points that must be allowed for in such comparisons is indicated.

Table B: Recommended Allowance for Sampling Error of the Difference in Percentage Points

(at 95 in 100 confidence level)*
Percentages near 20 or percentages near 80

Sample Size:	750	600	400	200
750	5			
600	5	6		
400	6	6	7	
200	8	8	8	10

*The chances are 95 in 100 that the sampling error is not larger than the figures shown.

Table C: Recommended Allowance for Sampling Error of the Difference in Percentage Points

(at 95 in 100 confidence level)*
Percentages near 50

Sample Size:	750	600	400	200
750	6			
600	7	7		
400	7	8	8	
200	10	10	10	12

*The chances are 95 in 100 that the sampling error is not larger than the figures shown.

Two tables are provided. Table B is for percentages near 20 or 80; Table C for percentages near 50. For percentages in between, the error to be allowed for is between those shown on the two tables.

Here is an example of how the tables would be used: Let us say that 50% of men respond a certain way and 40% of women respond that way also, for a difference of ten percentage points between them. Can we say with any assurance that the ten-point difference reflects a real difference between men and women on the question? The sample contains approximately six hundred men and six hundred women.

Since the percentages are near 50, we consult Table C, and since the two samples are about six hundred persons each, we look for the number in the column headed "600" that is also in the row designated "600". We find the number 7 here. This means that the allowance for error should be seven points, and that in concluding that the percentage among men is somewhere between three and seventeen points higher than the percentage among women we should be wrong only about 5% of the time. In other words, we can conclude with considerable confidence that a difference exists in the direction observed and that it amounts to at least three percentage points.

If, in another case, men's responses amount to 22%, say, and women's 24%, we consult Table B because these percentages are near 20. We look in the column headed "600" that is also in the row headed "600" and see that the number is 6. Obviously, then, the two-point difference is inconclusive.